W9-BVI-359

# The ^very Best of British

Mike Etherington

Effingpot Productions
www.effingpot.com

Published in the United Kingdom by:

**Effingpot Productions**
27 Higher Mead, Basingstoke,
Hampshire, RG24 8YL, UK
**www.effingpot.com**



A CIP record of this book is available from the British Library.

First printed September 2000

Layout and design by Gavin Bridger
www.gbdesign.co.uk

ISBN 0 9536968 1 2

# Contents



Words in *italics* are described elsewhere in the book and words in **bold** are the equivalent or closest American word.

# Slang

Chuck wondered what Charles could get for a penny in the john.

**Ace** - If something is ace it is **brilliant**. I used to hear it a lot in Liverpool. Kids thought all cool stuff was ace, or brill.

**Aggro** - Short for aggravation, it's the sort of thing you might expect at a football match. In other words - **trouble**! There is sometimes aggro in the cities after the pubs shut!

**All right?** - This is used a lot around London and the south to mean, **"Hello, how are you"**? You would say it to a complete stranger or someone you knew. The normal response would be for them to say "All right"? back to you. It is said as a question. Sometimes it might get expanded to "all right mate"? Mostly used by blue collar workers but also common among younger people.

**Anti-clockwise** - The first time I said that something had gone anti-clockwise to someone in Texas I got this very funny look. It simply means **counter-clockwise** but must sound really strange to you chaps! I think he thought I had something against clocks!

**Any road** - Up north (where they talk funny!!) instead of saying **anyway**, they say "any road"! Weird huh?

**Arse** - This is a word that doesn't seem to exist in America. It basically means the same as **ass**, but is much ruder. It is used in phrases like "pain in the arse" (a nuisance) or I "can't be arsed" (I can't be bothered) or you might hear something was "a half arsed attempt" meaning that it was not done properly.

**Arse about face** - This means you are doing something **back to front**.

**Arse over elbow** - This is another way of saying **head over heels** but is a little more descriptive. Usually happens after 11pm on a Saturday night and too many *lagers*! Some Americans say **ass over teakettle** apparently!

**Arse over tit** - Another version of *arse over elbow*, but a bit more graphic!

**Arsehole** - **Asshole** to you. Not a nice word in either language.

**Arseholed** - **Drunk**! Usually in the advanced stages of drunken stupor, someone would be considered completely arseholed. Never me, of course!

**As well** - You chaps say **also** when we would say "too" or "as well". For instance if my friend ordered a Miller Lite, I would say "I'll have one as well". I often heard people saying something like "I'll have one also". Of course in England you wouldn't say it at all for fear of embarrassment! You'd order a pint of *lager* instead!

**Ass** - Your backside, but mostly a **donkey**!

**Au fait** - Another one of those French expressions that have slipped into the English language. This one means to be **familiar** with something. I'd say at the end of reading all this you'd be au fait with the differences between American and English!

**Backy** - **Tobacco**. The sort you use to roll your own.

**Bang** - Nothing to do with your hair - this is a rather unattractive way of describing having **sex**. Always gets a smile from Brits in American hair dressers when they are asked about their bangs.

**Barmy** - If someone tells you that you're barmy they mean you have gone **mad** or **crazy**. For example you'd have to be barmy to visit England without trying *black pudding*!

**Beastly** - You would call something or somebody beastly if they were really **nasty** or **unpleasant**. Most people would consider you a snob or an upper class *git* if you used this word. People like Fergie can get away with it though.

**Bees knees** - This is the polite version of *the dog's bollocks*. So if you are in polite company and want to say that something was **fabulous**, this phrase might come in handy.

**Belt up** - For some reason I heard this quite a lot as a kid. It's the British for **shut up**.

**Bender** - I used to go out on a bender quite frequently when I was at university. Luckily bender doesn't only mean a **gay** man, it also means a *pub crawl* or a **heavy drinking session**. The sort of bender I went out on was the second kind. Obviously!

**Bespoke** - We say something is bespoke if it has been created especially for someone, in the same way that you say **custom**. For example a computer programme might be bespoked for a client, or you may order a bespoke *holiday*, where the travel agent creates an itinerary around your exact requirements.

**Best of British** - If someone says "The best of British to you" when you are visiting the UK, it simply means **good luck**. It is short for best of British luck.

**Biggie** - This is unusual. A biggie is what a child calls his **poo**! Hence the reason Wendy's Hamburgers has never really taken off in England - who would buy biggie fries? Yuck - I'm sure you wouldn't buy **poo fries**! The other meaning of Biggie is **erection**. It just gets worse!

**Bite your arm off** - This is not aggressive behaviour that a football fan might engage in. In fact it just means that someone is over **excited** to get something. For instance you might say that kids would bite your arm off for an ice cream on a sunny day.

**Bladdered** - This rather ugly expression is another way of saying you are **drunk**. The link is fairly apparent I feel!

**Blast** - An exclamation of surprise. You may also hear someone shout "blast it", or even "bugger and blast"!

**Blatent** - We use this word a lot to mean something is really **obvious**.

**Bleeding** - An alternative to the word *bloody*. You'll hear people say "bleeding hell" or "not bleeding likely" for example.

**Blimey** - Another exclamation of surprise. My Dad used to say "Gawd blimey" or "Gor blimey" or even "Cor blimey". It is all a corruption of the oath **God blind me**.

**Blinding** - If something is a blinding success - it does not mean that any eyes were poked out with sharp sticks - it means it was **fantastic**.

**Blinkered** - Someone who is blinkered is **narrow minded** or narrow sighted - they only see one view on a subject. It comes from when horses that pulled carriages wore blinkers to stop them seeing to the side or behind them which stopped them from being startled and only let them see where they were going.

**Bloody** - One of the most useful swear words in English. Mostly used as an exclamation of surprise i.e. "bloody hell" or "bloody Nora". Something may be "bloody marvellous" or "bloody awful". It is also used to emphasise almost anything, "you're bloody mad", "not bloody likely" and can also be used in the middle of other words to emphasise them. E.g. "Abso-bloody-lutely"! Americans should avoid saying "bloody" as they sound silly.

**Blooming** - Another alternative to the word *bloody*. You might hear someone say "not blooming likely" so that they don't have to swear.

**Blow me** - When an English colleague of mine exclaimed "Blow me" in front of a large American audience, he brought the house down. It is simply an exclamation of surprise, short for "Blow me down", meaning something like I am so surprised you could knock me over just by blowing. Similar to "Well knock me down with a feather". It is not a request for services to be performed.

**Blunt** - If a saw or a knife is not sharp we say it is blunt. It is also the way most of us speak! In America the knife would be **dull**.

**Bob's your uncle** - This is a well used phrase. It is added to the end of sentences a bit like **and that's it**! For example if you are telling someone how to make that fabulous banoffee pie you just served them, you would tell them to boil the condensed milk for three hours, spread it onto a basic cheesecake base, slice bananas on top, add some whipped *double cream*, another layer of banana and Bob's your uncle!

**Bodge** - We bodge things all the time here. I'm sure you do too! To do a bodge job means to do a quick and dirty. Make it look good for the next day or two and if it falls down after that - hey well we only bodged it! Applies to building, DIY, programming and most other things.

**Bogey** - **Booger**. Any variety, *crusty dragons* included!

**Bollocks** - This is a great English word with many excellent uses. Technically speaking it means **testicles** but is typically used to describe something that is no good (that's bollocks) or that someone is talking *rubbish* (he's talking bollocks). Surprisingly it is also used in a positive manner to describe something that is the best, in which case you would describe it as being "the dog's bollocks". Englishmen who live in America take great delight in ordering specialised registration plates for their cars using the letters B.O.L.L.O.X. Good eh?

**Bomb** - If something costs a bomb it means that it is really **expensive**. We say it when we see the price of insurance in the US, you could try saying it when you see how much jeans or *petrol* cost over here!

**Bomb** - If something goes like a bomb it means it is going **really well** or **really fast**. Or you could say an event went down like a bomb and it would mean that the people really enjoyed it. In the US the meaning would be almost exactly the reverse.

**Bonk** - Same meaning as *shag*. Means to **have sex**. E.g. "Did you bonk him/her?".

**Botch** - There are two expressions here - to botch something up or to do a botch job. They both mean that the work done was not of a high standard or was a clumsy patch. My Dad used to always tell me that workmen had botched it up and that he should have done the work properly himself.

**Bottle** - Something you have after twenty pints of lager and the curry. A lotta bottle! This means **courage**. If you have a lotta bottle you have **no fear**.

**Brassed off** - If you are brassed off with something or someone, you are **fed up**. **Pissed off** perhaps.

**Brill** - Short for "brilliant". Used by kids to mean **cool**.

**Bugger** - This is another fairly unique word with no real American equivalent. Like *bloody* it has many uses apart from the obvious dictionary one pertaining to rather unusual sexual habits. My father was always shouting "bugger" when he was working in the garage or garden. Usually when he hit his thumb or dropped a nail or lost something. Today we might use the sh** or the f*** words but bugger is still as common. The fuller version of this would be "bugger it". It can also be used to tell someone to get lost (bugger off), or to admit defeat (we're buggered) or if you were tired or exhausted you would be buggered. You can also call someone a bugger. When I won £10 on the lottery my mate called me a lucky bugger.

**Bugger all** - If something costs bugger all, it means that it costs **nothing**. Meaning it is cheap. If you have bugger all, it means you have nothing.

**Bum** - This is the part of your body you sit on. Your **ass**! It might also be someone who is down and out, like a *tramp*. You might also bum around, if you are doing nothing in particular, just hanging out. Finally to bum something means to **scrounge** it from someone.

**Bung** - To bung something means to **throw** it. For example a street trader might bung something in for free if you pay cash right now! Or you could say "bung my car keys over, *mate*".

**Bung** - A bung is also a **bribe**.

**Butchers** - To have a butchers at something is to **have a look**. This is a cockney rhyming slang word that has become common. The reason "butchers" means a look even though it doesn't rhyme is because it is short for "butchers hook" and "hook" of course, does rhyme.

**C of E** - The Church of England. Our official state church - of which the Queen is the head. In the US you call it **Episcopalian**.

**Chat up** - To chat someone up is to try and **pick them up**. If you spotted a *scrummy* girly in a bar you might try to chat her up. Or a girl might try and chat up a *chap*!

**Cheeky** - "Eee you cheeky monkey" was what my mother said to me all the time when I was a kid. Cheeky means you are **flippant**, have too much lip or are a bit of a *smart arse*! Generally you are considered to be a bit cheeky if you have an answer for everything and always have the last word. My licence plate on my MX5 (Miata in American) was CHEEKY, which most Texans thought was something to do with bottoms - wrong!!

**Cheerio** - Not a breakfast cereal. Just a friendly way of saying **goodbye**. Or in the north "*tara*" which is pronounced sort of like "churar".

**Cheers** - This word is obviously used when drinking with friends. However, it also has other colloquial meanings. For example when saying **goodbye** you could say "cheers", or "cheers then". It also means **thank you**. Americans could use it in English pubs, but should avoid the other situations as it sounds wrong with an American accent. Sorry!

**Cheesed off** - This is a polite way of saying you are **pissed off** with something.

**Chivvy along** - When I'm standing patiently in the checkout *queue* at Tesco I like to chivvy along the old ladies in front of me. If only they would stop *fannying around* and **hurry up**!

**Chuffed** - You would be chuffed to bits if you were really **pleased** about something.

**Clear off!** - This expression brings back memories of being a kid and stealing apples from people's gardens. Sometimes we would get caught and some old *bloke* would come out and shout "oi clear off you lot". It basically means **get lost**.

**Cobblers** - I have heard people say "what a load of cobblers" more than once. Maybe that's because I talk so much rubbish. An equivalent would be what a load of *bollocks*. It means you are **talking out of your butt** and has nothing to do with any kind of dessert!

**Cock up** - A cock up means you have made a **mistake**. It has nothing to do with parts of the male body.

**Cockney rhyming slang** - There are lots of words that make up cockney rhyming slang. These are basically rhyming words like "butchers hook" which means "look". If you are in London and you hear someone talk about a *Septic* they are probably talking about you - because it's short for

"Septic tank" which equals "*yank*", which is our word for an American. How do you like that!

**Codswallop** - Another one I heard a lot as a kid - usually when I was making up excuses for how the window got broken or why my dinner was found behind the sofa. My Dad would tell me I was talking a load of codswallop. American kids might be talking **baloney** under the same circumstances.

**Cor** - You'll often hear a Brit say "Cor"! It is another one of those expressions of surprise that we seem to have so many of. It will sometimes be lengthened to "Cor blimey" or "Cor love a duck", depending on where you are. "Cor blimey" is a variation of "Gawd blimey" or "Gor blimey". They are all a corruption of the oath "God blind me".

**Cracking** - If something is cracking, it means it is the **best**. Usually said without pronouncing the last "G". If a girl is cracking it means she is **stunning**.

**Cram** - Before a big exam you would be expected to cram. This simply means to **study hard** in the period running up to the exam.

**Crap** - The same word in both countries - but less rude here. I loved watching Brits being interviewed on US *chat shows* and embarrassing the interviewer when they said something was "total crap".

**Crikey** - Another exclamation of surprise. Some people say "Crikey Moses".

**Crusty dragon** - A **booger**. One of the really crispy ones.

**Daft** - My Dad used to call me a daft 'apeth which is short for a daft half penny (in old money). It basically means **stupid**.

**Dear** - If something is dear it means it is **expensive**. I thought Texan insurance was dear.

**Dicky** - Dicky rhymes with sicky and means you feel **sick**.

**Diddle** - To **rip someone off** or to **con** someone is to diddle them. When you visit England, check your change to make sure you haven't been diddled!

**Dim** - A dim person is **stupid** or *thick* or a *dim wit*.

**Dishy** - If someone is a bit of a dish or a bit dishy it means they are **attractive** or **good looking**.

**DIY** - This is short for **do it yourself** and applies not just to the DIY stores but also to anything that you need to do yourself. For example, if we get really bad service in a restaurant (oh, you noticed!) then we might ask the waiter if it is a DIY restaurant, just to wind them up.

**Do** - A **party**. You would go to a do if you were going to a party in the UK.

**Do** - If you go into a shop and say "do you do batteries?" it means "do you **sell** batteries".

**Do** - If you drive along a motorway in the wrong lane the police will do you. You could then tell your friends that you have been done by the police. **Prosecute** is another word for it!

**Doddle** - Something that is a doddle is a **cinch**, it's easy. Unlike ordering water in Texas with an English accent, which is definitely not a doddle!

**Dodgy** - If someone or something is a bit dodgy, it is **not to be trusted**. Dodgy food should be thrown away at home, or sent back in a restaurant. Dodgy people are best avoided. You never know what they are up to. Dodgy goods may have been *nicked*. When visiting Miami I was advised by some English chums that certain areas were a bit dodgy and should be avoided!

**Dog's bollocks** - You would say that something **really fantastic** was the dog's bollocks. I have no idea why - it has nothing to do with hounds and nothing to do with testicles!

**Dog's dinner** - If you make a real **mess** of something it might be described as a real dog's dinner. A bit like some joint Anglo-American approaches to Eastern Europe for example!

**Donkey's years** - Someone said to me the other day that they hadn't seen me for donkey's years. It means they hadn't seen me for **ages**.

**Drop a clanger** - When I asked a large lady on the *tube* if she would like my seat since she was so obviously pregnant, she took the seat then told me she was fat, not pregnant! Boy did I drop a clanger. You might **make a gaffe**. Either way it was horrendously embarrassing, especially as half the people on the *tube* had heard me!

**Duck** - In and around Leeds you will find older people might call you "duck" in the same way that they might call you "love" or "dear" in other places. Usually pronounced more like "dook", which rhymes with "book".

**Duff** - Anything that is duff is **useless, junk, trash**. It usually means that the object doesn't do the job it was intended for. Our last Prime Minister was pretty duff!

**Duffer** - Any person that is duff could be referred to as a duffer. The Prime Minister was a duffer.

**Dull** - You would say something that was no longer sharp was dull. We would say *blunt*. To us something is dull if it is **boring**. It can apply to things - like a *film* could be dull. It also applies to people - I can think of several people who are dull!

**Engaged** - When you ring someone and they are already on the phone you will get the engaged tone. In other words, they will be engaged. You would say you get the **busy** signal or the line is busy.

Charles was horrified at Chuck's personal problems.

**Excuse me** - This is a great one! It's what kids are taught to say when they belch in public. We are also taught to say "pardon me" if we fart out loud. Unfortunately in American "excuse me" means you are encroaching in someone's personal space and you say "pardon me" when you don't hear someone properly. Imagine our surprise when we discovered that actually Americans are not belching and farting all the time.

**Faff** - To faff is to **dither** or to *fanny around*. If we procrastinated when getting ready for bed, as kids, our Dad use tell us we were faffing around.

**Fagged** - If you are too lazy or tired to do something you could say "I can't be fagged". It means you can't be **bothered**.

**Fagging** - Fagging is the practice of making new boys at boarding schools into slaves for the older boys. If you are fagging for an older boy you might find yourself running his bath, cleaning his shoes or performing more undesirable tasks.

**Fancy** - If you fancy something then it means you **desire** it. There are two basic forms in common use - food and people. If you fancy a cake for example it means you like the look of it and you want to eat it. If you see someone of (hopefully) the opposite sex then you might fancy them if you liked the look of them and wanted to get to know them a little better!!!

**Fanny** - This is the word for a woman's **front bits**! One doesn't normally talk about anyone's fanny as it is a bit rude. You certainly don't have a fanny pack, or smack people on their fannys - you would get arrested for that! Careful use of this word in the UK is advised!

**Fanny around** - I'm always telling people to stop fannying around and get on with it. It means to **procrastinate**. Drives me mad!

**Fiddle sticks** - I have an old aunt who is much too well mannered to swear. So when the need arises for a swear word, she will substitute "fiddle sticks".

**Filch** - To filch is to **steal** or **pilfer**. The origin is apparently unknown.

**Fit** - Fit is a word that I have heard a lot recently - it seems to be making a comeback. A fit *bird* means a girl who is pretty **good looking** or tasty! A fit *bloke* would be the male equivalent.

**Flog** - To Flog something is to **sell** it. It also means to beat something with a whip, but when your wife tells you she flogged the old TV it is more likely she has sold it than beaten it (hopefully!).

**Fluke** - If something great happened to you by **chance** that would be a fluke. When I was a kid my Mum lost her engagement ring on the beach and only realised half way home. We went back to the spot and she found it in the sand. That was a fluke.

**Flutter** - I like to have a flutter on the horses. It means to have a **bet**, usually a small one by someone who is not a serious gambler.

**Fortnight** - **Two weeks**. Comes from an abbreviation of "fourteen nights". Hence terms like "I'm off for a fortnights *holiday*" meaning "I am going on a two week vacation".

**Full monty** - Since the movie has come out of the same name I have heard some odd Texan descriptions of what the full monty means. It really has nothing to do with taking your clothes off. It just means the **whole thing** or going the **whole way**. That's it. Clearly when applied to stripping it means not stopping at your underwear! The origins of the expression are still under discussion. There are many theories but no conclusive evidence at the moment.

**Full of beans** - This means to have **loads of energy**. It is a polite way of saying that a child is a maniac. I was often described as being full of beans as a kid and now it is my wife's way of telling me to keep still when she is trying to get to sleep. Strangely the same expression in some parts of the US means that you are exaggerating or talking *bollocks*!

**Gagging** - **Desperate**, in a fat slaggy kind of a way. Not nice.

**Gallivanting** - The dictionary says "to gad about", which probably doesn't help much! It means **fooling around** or **horseplay**.

**Gander** - When I was a kid, my Dad often used to go off for a gander when we were visiting a new town or village. It means to **look around**.

**Gen** - Gen means **information**. If you have the gen then you know what is going on.

**Gen up** - To **research a subject** or to **get some information**.

**Get lost!** - Politely translated as **go away**, this is really a mild way of telling someone to f*** off!

**Get stuffed!** - Even politer way to tell someone to *get lost* is to tell them to get stuffed. However, this is still not a nice thing to say to someone.

**Give us a bell** - This simply means **call me**. You often hear people use the word "us" to mean "me".

**Gobsmacked** - **Amazed**. Your gob is your mouth and if you smack your gob, it would be out of amazement.

**Good value** - This is short for good value for money. It means something is a **good deal**.

**Goolies** - If you have been kicked in the goolies, your eyes would be watering and you would be clutching your **balls**!

**Gormless** - A gormless person is someone who has absolutely no clue. You would say **clueless**. It is also shortened so you could say someone is a total gorm or completely gormy.

**Grem** - The form of *gob* meaning **to spit** something out. e.g. Did you see him grem? Yuck. Usually associated with that ghastly noise as the content of the lungs are coughed into the mouth before gremming can take place. Grem is also the word that describes the green lump that is created in the process. You might call it **hacking** up a **hacker**.

**Grub** - **Food**. Similar to *nosh*. I remember my Dad calling "grub's up", when dinner was ready as a kid. A grub is also an insect **larva**. Not usually eaten in England. Actually is available in some Australian restaurants!

Chuck was not looking forward to his first English grub.

**Gutted** - If someone is **really upset** by something they might say that they were gutted. Like when you are told that you have just failed your driving test!

**Haggle** - **Barter** and **negotiate** are other words for haggle. Most people that *wangle* stuff are usually quite good at haggling. I just learnt that in the USA you **dicker** over a price, particularly for used cars!

**Hanky panky** - Hanky panky - or "slap and tickle" as some older folks call it - would be **making out** in America.

**Hard** - After your 20 pints of *lager*, the curry or the *doner*, your average 20 year old feels hard. Since his male organ has no chance of working at this stage, hard clearly refers to something else - it means he is ready to fight anything or anybody or to take on any bet. This is the time to make fun of drunken lads by betting them they can't jump off the end of the pier, hang on to the back of a bus etc.

**Hard lines** - This is another way of saying hard luck or **bad luck**.

**Hash** - The thing you call a **pound sign**! Before you ask, yes it is also something you smoke - see *wacky backy*. Also to make a real hash of something means you really **screwed it up**.

**Have** - This one used to wind me up a treat in Texas. When we were in restaurants with friends, they would say to the waiter something like "Can I **get** a refill". And the waiter would go and get them a refill. No no no - that's completely wrong. It's "Can I HAVE a refill". Not GET! If you say "Can I GET a refill" in the UK, the waiter will give you a funny look and tell you where to go and GET it - yourself!

**Healthy** - **Healthful**. I'm not really sure if this is slang or whether the American use of healthful is the real alternative to the English "healthy". We talk about a healthy lifestyle and about healthy food. I never heard anyone say smoking was "unhealthful" in the US but I suppose that must exist too!

**Her Majesty's pleasure** - When visiting England, try to avoid being detained at Her Majesty's pleasure. This means being **put in prison** with no release date!

**Hiya** - Short for **hi there**, this is a friendly way of saying **hello**.

**Honking** - Honking is **being sick** or **throwing up**. Presumably this is a problem in New York where there are signs on the streets that say "No Honking".

**Horses for courses** - This is a common saying that means **each to his own**. What suits one person might be horrible for someone else. If my Dad was trying to understand why my brother had wanted to get his ear pierced he might say "Oh well, it's horses for courses I suppose"!

**How's your father?** - This is a very old term for **sex** which plays on our apparent British sensitivity. Rather than saying the actual "sex" word you could refer to having a bit of How's your Father, instead - nudge, nudge, wink, wink. The sort of old fashioned saying dragged up by Austin Powers.

**Hump** - If you have got the hump it means you are in a **mood**. If you are having a hump, it means you are **having sex**. Care is advised when you try using these words for the first time. It could be embarrassing!

**Hunky-dory** - My English dictionary tells me that hunky-dory means **excellent**. We would generally use it to mean that everything is **cool** and groovy, on plan, no worries and generally going well.

**I'm easy** - This expression means **I don't care** or **it's all the same to me**. Not to be confused with how easy it is to lure the person into bed!

**Irony/sarcasm** - The cornerstones of British humour. This is one of the biggest differences between the nations. The sense of humour simply doesn't translate too well.

**Jammy** - If you are really lucky or **flukey**, you are also very jammy. It would be quite acceptable to call your friend a jammy b****rd if they won the lottery.

**Jimmy** - Actually short for Jimmy Riddle. i.e. I'm off for a Jimmy Riddle. This is Cockney rhyming slang for **piddle**!

**John Thomas** - Yet another word for a blokes *willy*! I always felt a bit sorry for people who were actually called John Thomas. What were their parents thinking?

**Jolly** - You hear people use this in all sorts of ways, but basically it means **very**. So "jolly good" would mean **very good**. A common exception is where you hear people say "I should jolly well think so!" which is more to emphasise the point.

**Keep your pecker up** - This is one way of saying **keep your chin up**. Use with caution as in some places your pecker is also your *willy*!

**Kip** - A short **sleep**, forty winks, or a snooze. You have a kip in front of the *telly* on a Sunday afternoon.

**Knackered** - The morning after twenty pints and the curry, you'd probably feel knackered. Another way to describe it is to say you feel shagged. Basically worn out, good for nothing, **tired out**, knackered.

**Knob** - Yet another word for your *willy*.

**Knock off** - To knock something off is to **steal** it, not to copy it!

**Knock up** - This means to **wake someone up**. Although it seems to have an altogether different meaning in the USA! At one time, in England, a *chap* was employed to go round the streets to wake the workers up in time to get to work. He knew where everyone lived and tapped on the bedroom windows with a long stick, and was known as a "knocker up". He also turned off the gas street lights on his rounds. Another meaning of this phrase, that is more common these days, is to **make something** out of odds and ends. For example my Dad knocked up a tree house for us from some planks of wood he had in the garage, or you might knock up a meal from whatever you have hanging around in the fridge.

**Knockers** - Another word for **breasts**.

**Knuckle sandwich** - If somebody offers you a knuckle sandwich you'd be best to decline the offer and leave at the next convenient moment. It isn't some British culinary delight - they're about to **thump you in the face**.

**Leg it** - This is a way of saying **run** or **run for it**. Usually said by kids having just been caught doing something naughty. Well it was when I was a kid!

**Love bite** - You call them **hickies** - the things you do to yourself as a youngster with the vacuum cleaner attachment to make it look like someone *fancies* you!

**Lurgy** - If you have the lurgy it means you are **ill**, you have the **Flu**. Don't go near people with the lurgy in case you get it!

**Luvvly-jubbly** - Clearly another way of saying **lovely**. Made famous by the TV show Only Fools and Horses.

**-ly** - These are two letters that seem to be left off words in America. I never heard anyone say something was "really nice" or "really cool", they would say **real nice** and **real cool**. We would be sent to the back of the class for grammar like that!

**Mate** - Most chaps like to go to the pub with their mates. Mate means **friend** or *chum*.

**Momentarily** - As you come into land at an American airport and the announcement says that you will be landing momentarily, look around to see if anyone is sniggering. That will be the Brits! I never did figure out why they say this. Momentarily to us means that something will only happen for an instant - a very short space of time. So if the plane lands momentarily will there be enough time for anyone to get off? Weird!

**Morish** - Also spell "moreish", this word is used to describe desserts in my house, when a single helping is simply not enough. You need more! It applies to anything - not just desserts.

**Mug** - If someone is a bit of a mug, it means they are **gullible**. Most used car salesmen rely on a mug to show up so they can sell something!

**Mutt's nuts** - If something is described as being "the mutt's" then you'll know it is **fantastic** or **excellent**. "The mutt's" is short for "the mutt's nuts" which is clearly another way of saying the *"dog's bollocks"*! All clear now?

**Naff** - If something is naff, it is basically **uncool**. *Anoraks* are naff, *salad cream* is also naff. You could also use it to tell someone to naff off, which is a politer way of telling them to f*** off!

**Nancy boy** - If someone is being pathetic you would call them a nancy or a nancy boy. It is the opposite of being *hard*. For example in cold weather a nancy boy would dress up in a coat, hat, gloves and scarf and a hard guy would wear a t-shirt. It's also another word for a **gay** man.

**Nark** - If someone is in a nark, it means they are in a **bad mood**, or being grumpy. It's also the word for a **spy** or **informant**. For example a coppers nark is someone who is a police informant - which you might call a **stoolie** or **stool-pigeon**. The origin is from the Romany word, nak, meaning "nose".

**Narked** - In the UK you would say that someone looked narked if you thought they were in a bad mood. In the US you might say that someone was **pissed**. We definitely would not say that, as it would mean they were drunk!

**Nesh** - My Dad used to call me a nesh wimp when I was a kid and I wanted him to take me places in his car because it was too cold to go on my bike. He meant I was being **pathetic** or a bit of a *nancy boy*. He might have had a point!

**Nice one!** - If someone does something particularly impressive you might say "nice one"! to them. It is close the Texan **good job** that you hear all the time.

**Nick** - To nick is to **steal**. If you nick something you might well get *nicked.*

**Nicked** - Something that has been **stolen** has been nicked. Also, when a copper catches a burglar red handed he might say "you've been nicked"!

**Nookie** - Nookie is the same as *hanky panky.* Something you do with your *bird.*

**Nosh** - **Food**. You would refer to food as nosh or you might be going out for a good nosh up, or meal! Either way if someone has just cooked you some nosh you might want to call it something else as it is not the nicest word to describe it.

**Not my cup of tea** - This is a common saying that means something is **not to your liking**. For example if someone asked you if you would like to go to an all night rave, they would know exactly what you meant if you told them it was not exactly your cup of tea!

**Nowt** - This is Yorkshire for **nothing**. Similarly *owt* is Yorkshire for **something**. Hence the expression "you don't get owt for nowt". Roughly translated as "you never get something for nothing" or "there's no such thing as a free lunch".

**Nut** - To nut someone is to **head butt** them. Nutting is particularly useful when at a football match.

**Off colour** - If someone said you were off colour they would mean that you look **pale** and **ill**! Not quite the same as something being off colour in the US!

**Off your trolley** - If someone tells you that you're off your trolley, it means you have gone raving bonkers, **crazy**, **mad**!

**On about** - What are you on about? That's something you may well hear when visiting the UK. It means what are you **talking about**?

**On the job** - If you are on the job, it could mean that you are **hard at work**, or **having sex**. Usually the context helps you decide which it is!

**On the piss** - If you are out on the piss, it means you are out to **get drunk**, or to get *pissed*.

**On your bike** - A very polite way of telling someone to f*** off.

**One off** - A one off is a **special** or a **one time** event that is never to be repeated. Like writing this book!

**Owt** - This is Yorkshire for **something**. Similarly *nowt* is Yorkshire for **nothing**. Hence the expression "you don't get owt for nowt". Roughly translated as "you never get something for nothing" or "there's no such thing as a free lunch".

**Pants** - This is quite a new expression - I have no idea where it came from. Anyway, it is now quite trendy to say that something which is **total crap** is "pants". For instance you could say the last episode of a TV show was "total pants".

**Pardon me** - This is very amusing for Brits in America. Most kids are taught to say "pardon me" if they fart in public or at the table etc. In America it has other meanings which take us Brits a while to figure out. I thought I was surrounded by people with flatulence problems!

**Parky** - Either short for Michael Parkinson, a famous *chat show* host, or more likely a word to describe the weather as being **rather cold**!

**Pass** - This means **I don't know** and comes from the old TV show, Mastermind, where contestants were made to say "pass" if they did not know the answer to the question.

**Pavement pizza** - Well here the *pavement* is the sidewalk and a pavement pizza is a descriptive way of saying **vomit**. Often found outside Indian restaurants early on a Sunday morning.

**Peanuts** - I hated one of my summer jobs as a kid because it paid peanuts. The full expression is that if you pay peanuts, you get monkeys. It is a fairly derogatory way of saying that manual labour doesn't need to be bright and doesn't need a lot of pay. Typically these days peanuts means something is **cheap**. For example we would say the *petrol* in the USA is peanuts or costs peanuts. Compared to our prices it is.

**Pear shaped** - If something has gone pear shaped it means it has become a **disaster**. It might be preparing a dinner party or arranging a meeting, any of these things can go completely pear shaped.

**Piece of cake** - I remember saying it's a piece of cake in front of one of my American friends, who then started looking around for the cake! It means **it's a cinch**!

**Pinch** - This means to **steal** something. Though when you say "steal" it is a bit more serious than pinch. A kid might pinch a cake from the kitchen. A thief would steal something during a burglary.

**Pip pip** - Another out-dated expression meaning **goodbye**. Not used any more.

**Piss poor** - If something is described as being piss poor it means it is an **extremely poor** attempt at something.

**Piss up** - A piss up is a **drinking session**. A visit to the pub. There is an English expression to describe someone as disorganised which says that he/she could not organise a piss up in a brewery!

**Pissed** - This is a great one for misunderstanding. Most people go to the pub to get pissed. In fact the object of a *stag night* is to get as pissed as possible. Getting pissed means getting **drunk**. It does not mean getting angry. That would be getting pissed off!

**Pissing around** - **Fooling about**, in the sense of messing around or making fun or just being silly. Not terribly polite.

**Plastered** - Another word for **loaded**. In other words you have had rather too much to drink down your *local*. It has nothing to do with being covered with plaster though anything is possible when you are plastered.

**Porkies** - More cockney rhyming slang. Short for "porky pies", meaning "pork pies". Rhymes with **lies**. My Mum always used to tell me I was telling porkies! And she was right!

**Porridge** - Doing porridge means to **serve time** in prison. There was also a comedy TV series called Porridge about a prisoner starring Ronnie Barker of The Two Ronnies fame.

**Posh** - Roughly translates as **high class**, though if you look at Posh Spice there are clearly exceptions to the rule!

**Potty** - This isn't just the thing you sit a toddler on - if you are potty it means you are a little **crazy**, a bit of a looney, one card short of a full deck.

**Pound sign** - Ever wondered why Brits flounder when voicemail messages say to press the pound sign? What on earth is the British currency doing on a phone anyway? Well, it isn't. To a Brit, the pound sign is the wiggly thing we use to denote the UK pound (or *quid*), in the same way you have a dollar sign.

**Prat** - Yet another mildly insulting name for someone. In fact, this one is a bit ruder than *pillock* so you probably wouldn't say it in front of Grandma.

**PTO** - This is an abbreviation for "please turn over". You will see it on forms in the UK where you would see the single word **over** in the USA.

**Puff** - If a Brit starts giggling in your local drugstore - it may be because they have just found a box of Puffs. To some of us Brits a puff is another word for a **fart**. Stems from the cockney rhyming slang, to puff a dart.

**Puke** - To puke is to **vomit** or to be **sick**. You may also hear someone say "you make me puke" - though I hope not! That would mean "you make me sick".

**Pukka** - This term has been revived recently by one of our popular young TV chefs. It means **super** or **smashing**, which of course is how he describes all his food.

**Pull** - Me and the lads used to go to the disco when we were on the pull. It means **looking for *birds***. Of course, it works the other way round too. The ladies may also be on the pull, though probably a bit more subtly than the *chaps*!

**Pussy** - This is what we call our **cat**, as in "pussy cat", or in the fairytale, Puss in Boots. So if you have a Brit neighbour who asks if you have seen their pussy - try to keep a straight face and think back the last time you saw their cat!

**Put a sock in it** - This is one way of telling someone to **shut up**. Clearly the sock needs to be put in their loud mouth!

**Put paid to** - This is an expression which means **to put an end to something**. For example you could say that rain put paid to the cricket match, meaning it stopped play.

**Quid** - A **pound** in money is called a quid. It is the equivalent to the **buck** or **clam** in America. A five pound note is called a fiver and a ten pound note is called a tenner.

**Quite** - When used alone, this word means the same as **absolutely**!

**Rat arsed** - Yet another term for **drunk**, *sloshed* or *plastered*. You might say **loaded**. In the UK, loaded is a men's magazine that covers sex and football.

**Read** - If someone asks you what you read at *university*, they mean what was your **major** at school.

**Really** - This is one of those words where you say almost the same thing as us, but just can't be *fagged* to finish it off. The word is "really", not **real**. You say things like it's real hot, something's real cool, a baby is real cute. If we said that we would be sent to the back of the class for our grammar - or lack of it!

**Redundancy** - If you are made redundant it means you are **laid off**.

**Reverse the charges** - When you want to *ring* someone up and you have no money you can call the operator and ask to reverse the charges in the UK. In the US you would **call collect**.

**Right** - I'm feeling right *knackered*. That would mean you were feeling **very** tired.

**Ring** - You would ring someone on the phone not **call** them, in the UK. Try saying "give me a ring" to the next Brit you meet. This does not work well in reverse. I asked someone in a shop to ring me up and he dragged me to the till and pulled my head across the scanner!

Chuck was a little nervous about Charles ringing him up.

**Roger** - Same kind of problem that Randy has here, except we have people called Roger and no Randys. You will see a strange smile on the face of a Brit every time Roger the Rabbit is mentioned!! To roger means to have your wicked way with a lady. My Oxford English Dictionary says **to copulate**. You might say **screw**.

**Round** - When you hear the words "your round" in the pub, it means it is your turn to **buy the drinks** for everyone in the group - nothing to do with the size of your tummy! Since beers are more and more expensive these days, the art of buying the rounds has developed into ensuring you buy the first one before everyone has arrived, without being obvious!

**Row** - Rhymes with "cow" this means an **argument**. You might hear your Mum having a row with your Dad, or your neighbours might be rowing so loud you can hear them!

**Rubbish** - The stuff we put in the *bin*. **Trash** or **garbage** to you. You might also accuse someone of talking rubbish.

**Rugger** - This is short for rugby. It is a contact sport similar to your **football** but played in muddy fields during winter and rain. Not only that, but the players wear almost no protection!

**Rumpy pumpy** - Another word for *hanky panky*, or a bit of *nookie*! Something two consenting adults get up to in private! Theoretically!

**Sack/sacked** - If someone gets the sack it means they are **fired**. Then they have been sacked. I can think of a few people I'd like to sack!

**Sad** - This is a common word, with the same meaning as *naff*. Used in expressions like "you sad b***ard".

**Scrummy** - This is a word that would be used to describe either some food that was particularly good (and probably sweet and fattening). Or it could also be used to describe an attractive girl, if you were a guy. The reverse is also true!

**Send-up** - To send someone up is to **make fun** of them. Or if something is described as being a send-up it is equivalent to your **take-off**. Like Robin Williams does a take-off on the British accent - quite well actually!

**Shag** - Same as *bonk* but slightly less polite. At seventies parties watch the look of surprise on the Englishman's face when an American girl asks him if he would like to shag. Best way to get a Brit to dance that I know! You can even go to shagging classes!

**Shagged** - Past tense of *shag*, but also see *knackered.*

**Shite** - This is just another way of saying **shit**. It is useful for times when you don't want to be overly rude as it doesn't sound quite as bad!

**Shitfaced** - If you hear someone saying that they got totally shitfaced it means they were out on the town and got steaming **drunk**. Normally attributed to *stag nights* or other silly events.

**Shufti** - Pronounced shooftee, this means to take a **look** at something, to take a *butchers*. It's an old Arabic word, picked up by British soldiers during World War II, in North Africa.

**Skew-whiff** - This is what you would call **crooked**. Like when you put a shelf up and it isn't straight we would say it is all skew-whiff.

**Skive** - To skive is to **evade** something. When I was a kid we used to skive off school on Wednesdays instead of doing sports. We always got caught of course, presumably because the teachers used to do the same when they were fourteen!

**Slag** - To slag someone off, is to **bad mouth** them in a nasty way. Usually to their face.

**Slapper** - A slapper is a female who is a bit loose. A bit like a *slag* or a *tart*. Probably also translates into **tramp** in American.

**Slash** - Something a *lager lout* might be seen doing in the street after his curry - having a slash. Other expressions used to describe this bodily function include; siphon the python, shake the snake, wee, **pee**, piss, piddle and having a *jimmy*.

**Sloshed** - Yet another way to describe being **drunk**. Clearly we need a lot of ways to describe it since getting *plastered* is a national pastime.

**Smarmy** - Another word for a **smoothy**, someone who has a way with the ladies for example. Usually coupled with "git" - as in "what a smarmy git". Not meant to be a nice expression, of course.

**Smart** - When *we* say someone is smart, we are talking about the way they are dressed - you might say they look **sharp**. When *you* say someone is smart you are talking about how intelligent or clever they are.

**Smashing** - If something is smashing, it means it is **terrific**.

**Smeg** - This is a rather disgusting word, popularised by the TV show, Red Dwarf. Short for smegma, the dictionary definition says it is a "sebaceous secretion from under the foreskin". Now you know why it has taken me 3 years to add it in here. Not nice! Rather worryingly smeg is also the name of a company that makes ovens!!!

**Snap** - This is the name of a card game where the players turn cards at the same time and shout "snap" when they match. People also say "snap" when something someone else says has happened to them too. For example when I told somebody that my *wallet* was stolen on holiday, they said "snap", meaning that theirs had too!

**Snog** - If you are out on the *pull* you will know you are succeeding if you end up snogging someone of the opposite sex (or same sex for that matter!). It would probably be referred to as **making out** in American, or serious kissing!

**Snookered** - If you are snookered it means you are up the famous creek without a paddle. It comes from the game of snooker where you are unable to hit the ball because the shot is blocked by your opponent's ball.

**Sod** - This word has many uses. My father always used to say "oh sod!" or "sod it!" if something went wrong and he didn't want to swear too badly in front of the children. If someone is a sod or an "old sod" then it means they are a bit of a **bastard** or an old *git*. "Sod off" is like saying "piss off" or "get lost" & "sod you" means something like "f*** off". It also means a chunk of lawn of course. You can usually tell the difference!

**Sod all** - If you are a waiter in America and you serve a family of Brits, the tip is likely to be sod all or as you would call it - **nothing**. Because we don't know about tipping.

**Sod's law** - This is another name for **Murphy's law** - whatever can go wrong, will go wrong.

**Sorted** - When you have **fixed a problem** and someone asks how it is going you might say "sorted". It's also popular these days to say "get it sorted" when you are telling someone to get on with the job.

**Speciality** - This is another one where you chaps drop your "I". when I first saw **specialty** written down in the US I thought it was a mistake. But no! We love our I's!

**Spend a penny** - To spend a penny is to **go to the bathroom**. It is a very old fashioned expression that still exists today. It comes from the fact that in ladies *loos* you used to operate the door by inserting an old penny.

**Splash out** - If you splash out on something - it means you throw your senses out the window, get out your credit card and **spend far too much money**. You might splash out on a new car or even on a good meal.

**Squidgey** - A chocolate cream cake would be squidgey. It means to be **soft** and, well, squidgey!

**Squiffy** - This means you are feeling a little **drunk**. Some people also use it to mean that something has **gone wrong**.

Chuck wondered what Charles could get for a penny in the john.

**Starkers** - Avoid being seen starkers when visiting England. It means stark **naked**.

**Stiffy** - Yet another word for **erection**.

**Stone the crows** - This is an old expression with the same meaning as "Cor *blimey*".

**Stonker** - This means something is huge. Looking at the burger you might say "*blimey* what a stonker". It is also used to refer to an **erection**! Clearly English modesty is a myth!

**Stonking** - This weird word means **huge**. You might say "what a stonking great burger" if you were in an American burger joint.

**Strop** - If someone is **sulking** or being particularly miserable you would say they are being stroppy or that they have a strop on. I heard an old man on the train tell his wife to stop being a stroppy cow.

**Stuff** - A recent headline in the New Statesman read "stuff the millennium". Using stuff in this context is a polite way of saying "**f******* the millennium". Who cares! Stuff it! You can also say "stuff him" or "stuff her" meaning they can *sod off*.

**Suss** - If you heard someone saying they had you sussed they would mean that they had you **figured out**! If you were going to suss out something it would mean the same thing.

**Sweet fanny adams** - This means **nothing** or *sod all*. It is a substitute for "sweet f*** all". It is also shortened further to "sweet F A".

**Swotting** - Swotting means to **study hard**, the same as *cram* does. Before exams we used to swot, not that it made any difference to some of us. If you swotted all the time, you would be called a swot - which is not a term of endearment!

**Ta** - We said "ta" as kids in Liverpool for years before we even knew it was short for **thanks**.

**Table** - We use this word in exactly the opposite way. To us a motion is tabled when it is brought to the table, or suggested for consideration. You table a motion when it is left for a later date.

**Taking the biscuit** - If something really takes the biscuit, it means it **out-does** everything else and cannot be bettered. Some places in America they said **takes the cake**.

**Taking the mickey** - *See taking the piss.* Variations include "taking the mick" and "taking the Michael".

**Taking the piss** - One of the things Americans find hardest about the Brits is our sense of humour. It is obviously different and is mainly based on irony, sarcasm and an in-built desire to take the piss. This has nothing to do with urine, but simply means **making fun** of someone.

**Talent** - Talent is the same as *totty*. Checking out the talent means looking for the sexy young girls (or boys I suppose).

**Tara** - Pronounced "churar", this is another word for *cheerio* or **goodbye**. Cilla Black, a *scouse* TV presenter has probably done most to promote the use of this word as she says it all the time on her programmes.

**Throw a spanner in the works** - This is an expression that means **to wreck something**.

**Tickety-boo** - If something is **going well** with no problems we would say it is tickety-boo.

**Tidy** - Apart from the obvious meaning of **neat**, tidy also means that a woman is a looker, **attractive** or sexy.

**To** - We go to school from ages 5 to 18. You might go to school from ages 5 **thru** 18. We don't say **thru** in that context at all. If we did though, we would say "through"!

**Todger** - As if we don't have enough of them already, this is yet another word for your *willy*, or **penis**.

**Toodle pip** - This is an old expression meaning **goodbye**. However, I only hear it when Americans are doing impressions of Brits as it has fallen into disuse, along with steam trains and gas lights.

**Tool** - Yet another word for your *willy* or **penis**. You'd think we were obsessed.

**Tosser** - This is another word for *wanker* and has exactly the same meaning and shares the same hand signal. Unfortunately my house in Texas was in Tossa Lane, which was a problem when telling older members of the family where to write to me!

**Totty** - If a chap is out looking for totty, he is looking for a nice **girl** to chat up. There is an Italian football player called Totti - which is pronounced the same. It's really funny hearing the commentators when he gets the ball saying "it's Totty for Italy". It sounds like some beautiful Italian girlies have invaded the pitch.

**TTFN** - Short for "ta ta for now". Which in turn means **goodbye**! Said by older folks and one Radio Two DJ in particular.

**Twat** - Another word used to insult someone who has upset you. Also means the same as *fanny* but is less acceptable in front of your grandmother, as this refers to parts of the female anatomy.

**Twee** - Twee is a word you would generally hear older people say. It means **dainty** or **quaint**. A bit like the way you chaps think of England I suppose.

**U** - A letter used far more in British. It is in words like colour, favour, labour etc. I think this is why UK keyboards have 102 characters on them instead of your 101, or is it because they have a *pound* sign on them?

**Uni** - Short for university, we would say we went to uni like you would say you went to **school**. School here is just for kids.

**Wacky backy** - This is the stuff in a joint, otherwise known as **pot** or **marijuana**!

**Waffle** - To waffle means to **talk** on and on about nothing. It is not something you eat. Americans often think that Brits waffle on about the weather. The truth of course is that our news reports last 60-120 seconds and the weather man is not hyped up to be some kind of superstar as he is on the TV in the US. If you want to see an example of real waffle watch the weather channel in Texas where there is nothing to talk about other than it is hot and will remain so for the next 6 months. Another example is the ladies who waffle on about anything on the Home Shopping Network. They would probably be classed as professional wafflers!

**Wangle** - Some people have all the luck. I know some people that can wangle anything; upgrades on planes, better rooms in hotels. You know what I mean.

**Wank** - This is the verb to describe the action a *wanker* participates in.

**Wanker** - This is a derogatory term used to describe someone who is a bit of a **jerk**. It actually means someone who masturbates and also has a hand signal that can be done with one hand at people that cannot see you shouting "wanker" at them. This is particularly useful when driving.

**Waz** - On average, it seems that for every pint of lager you need to go for a waz twice! A complete waste of time in a serious drinking session. It means **wee** or **pee**.

**Well** - Well can be used to accentuate other words. for example someone might be "well hard" to mean he is a **real man**, as opposed to just "*hard*". Something really good might be "well good". Or if you were really really pleased with something you might be "well chuffed". Grammatically it's appalling but people say it anyway.

**Welly** - If you give it welly, it means you are **trying harder** or **giving it the boot**. An example would be when accelerating away from lights, you would give it welly to beat the guy in the mustang convertible in the lane next to you. Welly is also short for Wellington boots, which are like your **galoshes**.

**Whinge** - Whingers are not popular in any circumstance. To whinge is to **whine**. We all know someone who likes to whinge about everything.

**Willy** - Another word for **penis**. It is the word many young boys are taught as it is a nicer word than most of the alternatives. Some people also use it for girls as there are no nice alternatives. Hence "woman's willy". Also used by grown ups who don't wish to offend (this word is safe to use with elderly Grandparents).

**Wind up** - This has a couple of meanings. If something you do is a "wind up" it means you are **making fun** of someone. However it you are "wound up" it means you are **annoyed**.

**Wobbler** - To throw a wobbly or to throw a wobbler means to **have a tantrum**. Normally happens when you tell your kids they can't have an ice cream or that it's time for bed.

**Wonky** - If something is shaky or **unstable** you might say it is wonky. For example I changed my chair in a restaurant recently because I had a wonky one.

**Write to** - When visiting the US one can't help noticing that you **write** each other. You don't "write to" each other. Here it would be grammatically incorrect to say "write me" and you would be made to write it out 100 times until you got it right.

**Yakking** - This means **talking incessantly** - not that I know anyone who does that now!

**Yonks** - "Blimey, I haven't heard from you for yonks". If you heard someone say that it would mean that they had not seen you for **ages**!

**Zed** - The last letter of the alphabet. The English hate saying **zee** and only relent with names such as ZZ Top (Zed Zed Top does sound a bit stupid!).

**Zonked** - If someone is zonked or zonked out, it means they are totally *knackered* or you might say **exhausted**. When a baby has drunk so much milk his eyes roll to the back of his head, it would be fair to say he was zonked!

# Food & drink

Chuck was shocked that Charles wanted a spotted dick.

**99** - When you visit England, go up to the ice cream van and ask for a 99. You will get a cone filled with soft ice cream and a Cadbury's *flake* - a long crumbly stick of chocolate. Mmmm!

**Afters** - "What's for afters?" When you hear a kid say that they are asking what is for **dessert**. Nothing if they didn't eat their liver and greens!

**Aubergine** - **Eggplant** to you.

**Bacon** - You also have bacon, but one of the things I missed was British bacon. Not the fact that it comes from Britain, more the choice. You seem to have one choice - bacon. We have back, throughcut, streaky, smoked, green and dry cured. The one we call "streaky" is the cheapest as there is almost no meat on it. It is the closest to the bacon you have in the US. The most expensive is back, as it is almost all meat. Your bacon is nice and crisps up, but for the country that likes choice, it's odd that there is none.

**Banger** - The good old British banger is bigger and fatter than the American breakfast link **sausage**. It is served for dinner with fried onions and gravy, in batter as *toad in the hole* or for breakfast with eggs, back bacon, mushrooms, *black pudding*, fried potatoes, grilled tomatoes, toast and marmalade. There are also many regional sausages that combine different meats, herbs and spices. And don't forget good old bangers and *mash*.

**Bap** - A soft round roll, lightly floured. These are like **hamburger buns** in America, but also eaten as sandwiches. Yummy with bacon and egg oozing out!

**Barbie** - Apart from being a doll, the barbie is the **grill**. Either charcoal or gas fired, it's what we cook our dinner on in the 2 days that makes up a good British summer. It's full name is the **barbeque**. So when we say barbie or BBQ we are talking about the cooker itself not the food. If you have people around you would call the event a BBQ as well.

**Beer** - Normally called *bitter*, this is the most popular alcoholic beverage of the UK male drinking population. It is served in *pints* at just under room temperature (*real ales*, however are served AT room temperature). Real ales are non carbonated beers made from hops and barley.

**Beer mat** - Pubs always serve beer on a little card **coaster** which advertises the brewery or beer. They make great frisbees and are used for several pub games/jokes/tricks. You'll have to come and visit to find out more.

**Beetroot** - This is called **beet** or **beets** in America. Here they come ready cooked normally in a little jar or in a bucket in street markets. Actually quite scrummy!

**Best** - "A pint of best please landlord". You should walk into a British pub and say this at the bar in your best British accent. After telling you that "you're not from round here" you will be served with a pint of fine **British ale**. You might find it a little warm, but it grows on you.

**Bevvy** - If someone asks you if you want to come out for a bevvy, they are asking you to the *pub* for a **beer**. Bevvy is just short for beverage, but in this context the beverage in question is obviously of the alcoholic nature!

**Bickie** - Short for *biscuit*. Usually said by kids and means **cookie** where you live.

**Biscuit** - **Cookie** in America. Though the large home-made chocolate chip type things would also be referred to as cookies in England. We also use the word "biscuit" to mean **cracker**, for instance you will see "biscuits for cheese" in the supermarkets, which are assortments of crackers.

**Bitter** - Bitter is what we call ***beer***. However, this is not what you call beer - we call that *lager*. Beers are the dark ales that are so popular amongst British drinkers. Served a little below room temperature, but not cold like yours.

**Black pudding** - Missed by Brits in America, thin or thick black pudding is one of the staples of a cooked breakfast. Looking like a black sausage it is made from pigs blood and fat. Sounds horrid, but like *faggots*, you should try it before passing judgement!

**Blancmange** - Blancmange is **custard** that has been made thick, and allowed to set. It is generally served as one of the layers in a trifle. The bottom layer would be sponge cake soaked in jelly, then some fruit, then the blancmange, then a layer of whipped *double cream* and finally a chocolate *flake* crumbled over the top. Yummy!

**Brown bread** - In cheap restaurants the choice of bread may be "white" or "brown". This is our equivalent of white or **wheat**. If you asked for "wheat" you'd get a strange look.

**Brown sauce** - If you are eating all day breakfast or something similar in a *pub*, you are likely to be asked if you would like brown sauce. It is pretty much like **steak sauce**, except the last thing we would put it on is a steak - yuck! We put it on things like cooked breakfast, which is probably just as disgusting to you.

**Bubble & squeak** - No, this isn't what happens to you when you drink too much. Bubble & squeak is an old English breakfast dish made from frying up left over **greens and potato**.

**Bucks fizz** - Apart from being a terrible pop group, bucks fizz is a drink made from ruining champagne with orange juice - **mimosa** to you.

**Buns** - Fruit buns are made by aunties and grandmas and often served with a *cuppa*. It is perfectly acceptable to say "Mmmmm, nice buns Grandma".

Charles couldn't take his eyes off Grandma's buns.

**Butty** - A butty is a **sandwich**. The most famous butty is the chip butty. The perfect chip butty (invented in Liverpool) consists of two fairly large slices from a large white loaf, liberally buttered, layered with *chips* (salt and vinegar optional) and smothered in *tomato sauce*.

**Candyfloss** - **Cotton candy**. The same horrible sugar based fluff that you get at *fairs* and *carnivals*. Kids love it and mums hate it.

**Canteen** - This is a **cafeteria** to you chaps. Not something a soldier drinks out of!

**Castor sugar** - This is white sugar that is somewhere between icing sugar and granulated sugar in texture. It is very finely granulated sugar, ideal for things like meringues, where granulated is too coarse and icing is totally unsuitable (I tried it once!!). In Texas it is called **superfine sugar**.

**Chip butty** - We grew up on these in Liverpool. They are sandwiches made from white bread, buttered and filled with piping hot *chips* and cold *tomato sauce*!

**Chip shop** - Abbreviation for *fish and chip shop*. Also known as the chippy or chipper in some places.

**Chipolata** - This is a small **pork sausage**. About the size of those served with breakfast in places like Denny's and IHOP. Not as popular as the fat old British banger. Chipolata is also a term used by women when they are winding up their husbands about their unimpressive manhood. In this instance the emphasis is usually on the "small" sausage.

**Chips** - **Fries** to you. *Fish and chips* is still a favourite in Old Blighty. Whilst government health restrictions prevent them from being served in newspaper any more, they still taste best from the bag, liberally dosed in salt and malt vinegar. Not to be confused with french fries, which are weedy little poncey things for girlies!

**Cider** - In some parts of south west England, Cider is more popular than beer. It is made from the juice of apples, allowed to ferment and is generally more alcoholic than most beers. Around Devon and Somerset, seasoned cider drinkers are easily spotted with their distended bellies and reddened ears, cheeks and noses. Cider is famous for rotting your guts!

**Clingfilm** - Unless you saw the Full Monty, clingfilm is used to wrap food to keep it fresh. **Plastic wrap** in America. Wrapping it around your stomach is actually NOT normal in the UK!!!

**Clotted cream** - This cream looks a bit scary at first. It is yellow and crusty on top. It is thicker than *single cream* or *double cream* and totally delicious. It is served in blobs with cakes or spread on *scones*. You can ask Grandma if you can spread some on her buns quite safely! (Avoid this in America, of course).

**Cocktail stick** - The little wooden sticks you get in America when you leave most restaurants! Here in the UK that practice isn't very common. It seems as if it is more polite here to wander around with teeth full of spinach than it is to pick your teeth with a **toothpick** in public. I like the way people in the US do it at the table while they are still talking to you, but to hide it they put one hand in front of their mouth. Mmmm very attractive!

**Cordial** - Cordial or *squash* in the UK is a concentrated drink, mostly for kids. Just add water. If you are a total wimp you can try adding lime or blackcurrant cordial to a pint of *lager*.

**Coriander** - **Cilantro**. It took a while to figure out why coriander wasn't available in supermarkets! Now we know! This applies to the fresh sort in particular.

**Cornflour** - **Corn starch** to you.

**Cornish pasty** - Nothing beats a proper pasty. Sadly these days they are harder to find. Many outlets sell what they call "pastys" but they are cheap and nasty imitations. A real pasty from Cornwall, is a pastry in the shape of a half circle, filled with spiced meat and potatoes. In the old days they also had apple at one end and they were tossed down the tin mines for the miners to eat for lunch. There is still a lot of rivalry in Cornwall about who makes the best pastys and a good one is worth searching for - a meal in itself.

**Courgette** - **Zucchini**. Asking for a zucchini in England will probably get you a puzzled look.

**Crackling** - The skin of the pork joint, scored with a knife, rubbed with salt and roasted so that it crunches around the outside of the meat. Fabulous!

**Cream Tea** - This is something you should definitely try when you visit England, particularly if you are visiting the little villages of Cornwall or the West Country. A real cream tea consists of a pot of tea, some fresh warm *scones* that you spread with homemade strawberry *jam* and top with thick, yellow, *clotted cream*. Delicious!

**Crisps** - Salt and vinegar, cheese and onion, beef, smoky bacon. Crisps are called **chips** in America.

**Crispy duck** - One thing I really missed in America was crispy duck. In almost every chinese restaurant in England this is on the menu. It is marinated roasted duck that is smashed up at the table and served in tiny, almost see-through pancakes with hoi-sin sauce and shredded cucumber and *spring onions*. Eaten like Fajitas it is fantastic. Not to be confused with Peking Duck, which is usually the next item on the menu here.

**Crumpet** - One of the oldest traditions in English foody fads is the crumpet. A cratered flat cake. Toasted and covered in butter, so that it drips into the holes, the crumpet is enjoyed at tea on a Sunday, during the winter. It is about the size and shape of an *English muffin* (itself recently introduced to the UK and unheard of by most Brits!). Crumpet also has another meaning. Men might refer to women as a bit of crumpet, or they might fancy some crumpet tonight. You probably get the drift!

**Cuppa** - Cup of Tea. Served at 4pm, sometimes with tea cakes, *crumpets*, *biscuits* or cakes. My favourite is a real *cream tea* which is a pot of tea with *scones*, *clotted cream* and strawberry *jam*. Tea is also served in bed at the weekends when you wake up. Mmmmmm!

**Curry** - England has more than it's fair share of Indian restaurants. Anything from a korma or a bhuna to a madras or a vindaloo are amongst the favourite curries. Curry houses are one of the few places that serve alcohol (*lager*) after the pubs shut. Therefore it is very popular, after your 10 pints of *lager*, to pop next door to the curry house for 10 more pints, some poppadoms and a good curry. This mixture is perfect for churning out the infamous *pavement pizza*. Use your imagination!

**Digestive biscuit** - These are one of the most boring biscuits you can buy in England. However, they are popular because they make the perfect cheesecake base. The nearest thing I found in Texas was Graham Crackers which are not a patch on digestives.

**Dish up** - Sit at the table everyone - I'm about to dish up. This means you are about to **serve dinner**.

**Doner** - Short for a doner kebab. The closest thing in the US is a **gyro**. Kebabs in England, whether shish (meat on a skewer) or a doner (lamb on vertical spit), are served in split pitta bread with salad. There is a whole culture difference between the clean living shopping mall gyro and the greasy doner. Whilst the gyro is available all day and all evening and enjoyed by everyone, the doner is generally sold after 11pm in England to young males, after the pubs close and after 8 or so pints of *lager*. Usually served with extra hot fresh chilli sauce and on greaseproof paper so the oil is funnelled back onto your *trousers*, it is usually enjoyed standing up.

**Double cream** - This is even thicker than *single cream* and is also served with desserts, *tarts* etc. We didn't find cream this thick in Texas, even in dairy farms.

**English muffin** - No such thing. Nobody seems to know why these are called this. Until recently, they were not available in England. Even now that some supermarkets stock them, most Brits think they are things you get in America. And they think they are big fluffy things! Cause we're not big on muffins either.

**Entree** - **Appetizer**. You guys really got this one mixed up. You talk about the main course being the entree and the first course being the appetizer. Clearly this is the use of a French word, but sadly, in the wrong place. In France and the rest of Europe, the entree is the appetizer, not the main course. The clue is in the name!

**Faggot** - Never knock faggots until you have tried them! They are a traditional British delicacy. Made by many butchers, they are **meatballs** wrapped in a casing of intestine. Delicious! The best known commercial brand is Brains Faggots - eat them with *gravy*.

**Fairy cake** - This not a cake for effeminate men, it is a **cupcake**.

**Fillet** - A fillet steak in English is a **filet mignon** in American. Same thing and as far as I can tell, same price, 10 *quid* a pound in Tesco or 15 bucks a pound in Albertson's. Pronounced "Fill It".

**Fish and chip shop** - Since I was a kid and stopped off at the *chip shop* with the Boy Scouts after swimming, until tonight where I picked up a meal for wifey and I, the *chip shop* has been an important part of the British culinary experience. Mimicked badly on your side of the water nothing beats a good bag of cod'n'chips, some *mushy peas* and a *saveloy*. *Bloody* marvellous!

**Fish cake** - Fish cakes in the UK are served in restaurants rather like they are in the US, made from nice fish, with a little salad and a fancy berry sauce as a starter. However, ask most Brits what a fish cake is and they will tell you it is something you get at the *chip shop*, because it's easier to eat with your fingers than a piece of cod and cheaper too!

**Flake** - One thing I really missed was British chocolate. It's different to Hersheys. When we weakened, we sneaked down to Fiesta International Supermarket and splashed out on "The crumbliest, flakiest, milk chocolate in the world" as the TV *ad* says. Cadbury's Flake is fabulous - try some of our chocolate when you visit. You might like it!

**Garibaldi** - All kids know Garibaldi biscuits as "squashed fly biscuits". They are small hard biscuits with currants embedded in them that look just like squashed flies. Luckily they taste better than that.

**Gateau** - This is a **cake**, but not any old cake. A gateau should be large and rich and probably brimming with fresh cream. Normally served in slices on special occasions.

**Gherkin** - A gherkin is a **pickle** to you. Not as popular in England as they are in the US.

**Golden syrup** - This is something you don't appear to have in the US - it is a ridiculously thick syrup used for sticky puddings and desserts. The closest I found was **corn syrup**, which is a good alternative. Strangely it features in *treacle pudding*, which seems to have no *treacle* in it!

**Granary** - This is a kind of malted, **brown bread** with whole grains in it. Very popular here in Blighty and damned well worth trying.

**Gravy** - A brown sauce made from the meat juices when you roast a joint. It is never white, nor made from flour and milk. We call the gravy you find in the southern states *white sauce*.

**Grill** - We say grill when you say **broil**.

**Grub** - This is another word for **food** (hence *pub grub*) as well as being the larval stage of an insects development. Therefore care is required when ordering!

**Haggis** - One of the best known and most misunderstood Scottish inventions. Haggis is made from *offal* and grain and is held together in a sheep's stomach. It can be grilled, fried, or boiled whole. It is absolutely delicious and is traditionally served with neaps and tatties (turnips and mashed potato).

**Herb** - **Herb**. The only difference is we pronounce the "H". It got confusing when, having learnt to drop the "H" when talking about the food variety, I met someone called Herb and said "Hi Urb". apparently there is a little inconsistency here!

**Hob nobs** - One of the more popular British *biscuits*.

**Horlicks** - This **malted milk drink** has been around for years. It is supposed to make you relax in the evening and sleep well. Hence the old joke "Twelve children? Have you never heard of Horlicks?"

**Hot pot** - My Mum used to make good old Lancashire hot pot. Basically it is a kind of one-pot **stew** that is made with lamb with sliced potatoes on top, that go a bit crunchy. Yummy!

**HP sauce** - This is pretty close to your **A1 sauce**. The main difference is we would not dream of putting it on a steak, we put it on breakfast - cooked, that is (not cornflakes!!).

**Iced tea** - In England there was no such thing as iced tea. Tea is only drunk hot and Brits are quite adamant about the way they do it. As we left the UK in 1996 there were canned varieties of iced tea starting to appear in supermarkets but I doubt you'd get a glass if you asked for one in a restaurant. You'd probably get a blank stare. We brought about 50 customers to Texas on a business trip and when they arrived after a VERY long trip to the 100 degree Texan weather, the hotel kindly laid on a buffet with 50 glasses of iced tea already poured. Thinking this was some soft drink, and being extremely hot and bothered the customers all took big gulps and then simultaneously spat 50 mouthfuls of it across the table. That sort of explains what Brits think of iced tea. (It was very funny - you should have seen the catering manager's face).

**Icing sugar** - You call this **confectioner's sugar** or **powdered sugar**. When we worked in Kipling's cake factory as students we often got covered in icing sugar when the machines belched clouds of it into the air. An important lesson in removing it from your hair was to have a bath, NOT a shower as it turned into icing when mixed with water and the shower just could not provide enough water to get rid of it!

**Jacket potato** - **Baked potato** in America. Also referred to as potatoes in their jackets, meaning their skins, not little tuxedos!

**Jaffa cake** - These yummy little things are a little cake filled with orange jam and topped with chocolate. Very popular with kids.

**Jam** - **Jelly**. Not to be confused with *jelly* of course - which you call jell-o!

**Jellied eels** - In the east end of London, these are a local tradition and delicacy. As the name suggests they are simply eels, cooked and left to set in their own jelly. Yuck!

**Jelly** - **Jell-o** to you. Though jelly is not a brand name - it is the generic name for that rubbery stuff that kids like. Jell-o shots are not seen in the UK like they are in the US. I thought it was really odd to find it for sale near bars and generally adult type places. Soon found out why though!

**Joint** - Either something containing *wacky backy* that you smoke to get high, or a piece of **meat** that is roasted on a Sunday with roast spuds, roast parsnips, veggies and *gravy*. Like roast leg of pork and crackling. Mmmmmmmm!

Chuck was eager to visit Grandma for a Sunday joint.

**Kedgeree** - A wonderful dish of smoked haddock, eggs and rice. Still served in some hotels, generally for breakfast.

**Kipper** - A **smoked herring**. Kippers are very popular eaten hot with breakfast or cold with a salad.

**Lager** - Sort of what you call beer. Usually a bit stronger and drunk from pint glasses rather than bottles. Served cold, but not that cold. American beer is not normally considered a manly drink by British males. In the Epcot Centre in Florida, one of my American friends visited the "British Pub" where he ordered a pint of Guinness and his wife ordered a pint of "whatever was closest to American beer". The English waiter merrily brought his Guinness and for her - a pint of water!

**Lager lout** - This famous British invention is male, between 18 and 23 and usually visits foreign football matches to make trouble, beat people up and vandalise the place. Also available in other European flavours (e.g. Dutch).

**Lemonade** - Lemonade in England is a clear, sparkling, lemon flavoured drink that is either drunk as it is or added to *lager* to make *shandy*. **Seven-up** and **sprite** would both qualify as lemonade in England.

**Liver sausage** - I still remember my Mum cutting thick slices of liver sausage and grilling it with bacon and *black pudding* and serving it with eggs, tomatoes and sausages for breakfast - yummy! I have heard it called **liverwurst** in America.

**Marmite** - Described as "salty tractor grease" this spread is made from the yeast gunk they scoop out of beer vats when they are finished with them. You may have heard of Vegemite in Australia which is almost the same thing. Definitely an acquired taste. Usually used in sarnies with cheese.

**Mash** - Pie and mash, *bangers* and mash. All good pub favourites. Simply short for **mashed potato**.

**Mince** - In English this is **ground beef** (or other meat). Mincing is also the way that certain effeminate men walk!

**Mince pies** - At Christmas time we make mince pies. They are small pies filled with mincemeat and topped off with cream or served hot with brandy butter.

**Mincemeat** - Mincemeat is a sweet product made from dried fruit and suet (a dry form of beef fat) and is used as a filling for *mince pies*, eaten at Christmas with brandy butter.

**Mushy peas** - An English tradition. Mushy peas are reconstituted dried peas that go all mushy. They are often served with *fish and chips*, or on their own with mint sauce.

**Neat** - If you are in the pub and you ask for your drink neat, it means it comes with nothing added. You might ask for it **straight**.

**Normal** - When you order a soda in the US you often get asked if you would like "diet" or "**regular**". If we were asked the question at all here you would be asked "diet" or "normal". This generally applies to the times you would use regular. Slightly amusingly the question "diet or regular" to a Brit would translate into something like "are you on a diet or are you regular on the toilet". We say "regular" to mean going to the *loo* every day, so please be careful how you use the word in the UK.

**Nosh** - This is simply another word for **food**. If you were going out for some nosh it would mean you were going to get some lunch or dinner at a restaurant. Posh nosh is what you get at expensive restaurants.

**Nosh-up** - This means a **feast**.

**Off licence** - Beer, wine and spirits are sold in supermarkets in England, though the off licence still thrives. It is the place that you go to buy all of these items in the same way that you would from a **liquor store** in the US. Also called the offy.

**Offal** - In English supermarkets you will see a sign in the meat aisle with "offal" on it. In Texas it is referred to as **organ meat** - yuck! In the UK we love it. The most common offal is liver and kidney. My American friends tell me that offal is not eaten in the US. Maybe they should check out the ingredients of their hot dogs!

**Pancake roll** - Otherwise known as a spring roll here or **egg roll** in the US. No matter what you call them, if you buy one from a *take-away* you can be guaranteed it will pour boiling hot fat down your chin as you bite into it! Yikes!

**Parkin** - A **sweet heavy cake** made with *treacle.* Often served on *bonfire night.*

**Parsley sauce** - This is just a **white sauce** - like your southern gravy with chopped fresh parsley in it. Sometimes served with ham or fish.

**Parson's nose** - I have no idea why this is called the parson's nose, it is the **tail of the chicken** or turkey and very popular with Dads for no apparent reason. Not many parsons I know who would have their nose up there!

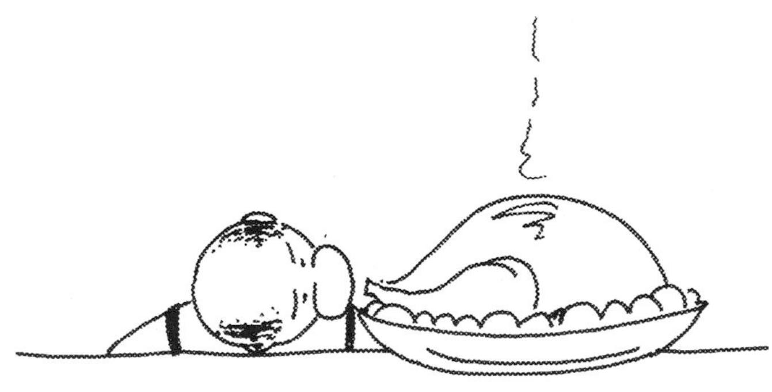

Chuck wonders where the rest of the parson is?

**Pastry base** - **Crust** to you.

**Pea fritter** - Well I just got back from the *chip shop* and realised I had forgotten to add pea fritters to this list. It is made from *mushy peas*, rolled into a ball, covered in batter and deep fried. Excellent as part of a calorie controlled diet!

**Peckish** - If you are a little peckish it means you are **hungry** and need to nibble at something.

**Perry** - Perry tastes a lot like our *cider*. That's because it is made the same way except instead of apples, they use pears. Just as alcoholic and just as likely to make you fall over.

**Pickle** - No such thing in America. Visit any English home and say "bring out the Branston" - they will bring you a jar of brown, lumpy, spicy pickle. It is made from vegetables, spices & vinegar and is quite thick. It is eaten with cold meats, cheeses and pies. There is even a less lumpy version for *sarnies*. Branston is the name of the market leader in pickle. Don't visit England without trying it.

**Pickled onions** - These little onions are a staple part of the British diet. Every kitchen has a jar in the cupboard or the fridge and many people still make their own. Peeled little **shallots in pickling vinegar** and eaten with cheese and salads. These days they also come with chilli and other hot spicy things to blow your head off.

**Pie** - This word is more of a subtle difference in usage. Unless specified otherwise, a pie would default to a meat pie with a pastry lid. Of course, we still have apple pies and the like. Pie's always have lids. No lid - no pie! We call that a *tart*.

**Pimms** - Another English tradition. Pimms is a liquor that you mix with *lemonade* in a tall glass with slices of apple, orange and cucumber and some fresh mint leaves. It is a summer, outside sort of drink that people drink at home and at the races, Wimbledon, Ascot, Henley etc. It is fairly alcoholic.

**Pint** - You would ask your mates if they wanted to come to the pub for a pint. In this instance it means any form of beer or cider that could be purchased in quantities of one pint. The British pint is bigger than the pint in the US. **20oz** rather than 16oz, demonstrating that not everything is bigger and better in Texas!

There was definitely something about English pints that appealed to Chuck.

**Plonk** - Normally you hear someone talking about cheap plonk. Under £3 would probably get you cheap plonk, you need to pay a bit more to get decent wine. Cheap plonk suggests that the **wine** is not only cheap, but nasty too.

**Pop** - **Soda**. Actually we don't really have a word for soda, we are more likely to ask if you want a coke, meaning any fizzy drink. In the north, you will hear people talking about pop or fizzy pop which has the same meaning as soda, but it is rarely used in other areas. "Pop" is also used frequently in Canada and in some parts of the US.

**Pork pies** - In central England, there is a little town called Melton Mowbray. The only notable thing about Melton is that it is the home of the very British pork pie. Even the Queen has been to the little pork pie shop in Melton. They are made from crusty pastry with a filling of minced pork. Cooked with secret ingredients. It is eaten cold with *pickle*.

**Pork scratchings** - In pubs, there are always bags of *crisps* and pork scratchings. In America they are called **pork rinds**.

**Porridge** - This has two meanings. The first is **cooked oatmeal** that you would have for breakfast. The second is **doing time in prison**.

**Pub grub** - Pubs that do food will often advertise "pub grub" outside on a sign. It just means **pub food**. These days lots of pubs do decent food, not just sausage, egg and chips!

Useful when travelling around the UK as we don't have restaurants lining the streets like so much of the US.

**Pudding** - **Dessert** of any type is called pudding. What you call pudding is called banana custard in England. There are also some brands of kids dessert called Instant Whip and Angel Delight which closely resemble American "pudding", but we don't have a generic term for these.

**Rasher** - You have to have a couple of back rashers with a proper English breakfast. You would call them **slices of bacon**.

**Rump steak** - This is what you call **sirloin steak**. And if that isn't confusing enough - our sirloin steak is your porterhouse!

**Runner beans** - **String beans** to you.

**Salad cream** - One of the worst British inventions has got to be salad cream. It is supposed to be a salad dressing of sorts but it is more like yellow ketchup with a sour vinegary flavour. The only saving grace is that it is pretty good in coleslaw.

**Sarny** - **Sandwich**. Sarnies again for lunch!

**Saveloy** - The saveloy is a rather odd kind of **sausage**. Similar to a long hot dog sausage, it is generally found in *fish and chip shops*, heated in hot water and served with *chips* as an alternative to fish (or in my case, an addition!)

**Savoury** - In some cafes and tea shops you might see savouries on the menu or the black board. This is just a term for **pastries** that are savoury rather than sweet. They might have cheese, or meat in them, like *Cornish pasties* for example.

**Scoff** - This word is both a verb and a noun, both related. If you were off home for some scoff you would be on your way for some **food**. However you might then scoff it down - meaning **to eat it**!

**Scones** - These look like your **biscuits** but must ONLY be eaten with *clotted cream* and strawberry *jam*. If you are ever lucky enough to encounter real scones (with or without currants), in England or on a British Airways flight, cut the scone in half and spread the *jam* on each half, top it off with the cream and enjoy it with a cup of tea. No other method is permitted or forgivable. Most arrests of American tourists are for eating scones the wrong way!

**Scotch egg** - Horrid, though they are, I actually like scotch eggs! They are hard-boiled eggs surrounded in a half-inch layer of sausage meat and coated in breadcrumbs and deep fried. Then you eat them cold at picnics!

**Scrumpy** - I grew up on scrumpy. It is **rough cider**. It tastes pretty harmless but after a pint or two stand back and wait for your legs to collapse. Best to buy it from a cider farm in Somerset or that end of the country. Though some pubs do sell something pretty close these days.

**Semi-skimmed** - **2%** to you! Took me ages to figure out that our semi-skimmed milk was the same as your 2% milk or **low fat milk**.

**Semolina** - Kids love semolina here like they love **cream of wheat** in the US. It's the same thing!

**Shandy** - Generally ***lager* and *lemonade***. However, bitter shandy and cider shandy are also popular, especially with drivers or at lunchtimes. (Hint for Brits - when explaining to a US barman how to make a shandy - don't ask for lager and lemonade - he won't have any idea what you are talking about and the result is likely to be disgusting. Ask for beer and sprite, then wait for the laughter and funny looks).

**Shepherds pie** - Originally made from leftovers, this is not a true pie, nor does it contain any shepherds! It is *mince*, either beef or lamb, cooked with some veggies and topped with mashed potato with cheese on top and grilled till brown. Can be quite nice but avoid being served this by any students.

**Simnel cake** - This is the traditional British **Easter cake**. It is a heavy fruit cake with a thick layer of marzipan right through the centre. There is marzipan on the top too plus usually balls or chicks made from marzipan decorating the top. Excellent with a *cuppa*.

**Single cream** - This cream is used for pouring on cakes and pies and is best served poured over apple pie. Single cream can be whipped to make it stiff for topping cheesecakes etc. The nearest thing to this in Texas is **heavy whipping cream**, sadly.

**Sirloin steak** - This is what you call **porterhouse**. And if that isn't confusing enough - our rump steak is your sirloin!

**Skimmed milk** - **Skim milk** in America. So what happened to the "ed" bit? It seems like a grammatical error to leave it off, but then you say things like "write me" instead of "write to me", which would also lose you marks in an English exam here. But then what would we know about English?

**Soldiers** - We dip soldiers in our soft boiled eggs. They are not actually men in uniform. They are **finger sized slices of toast**.

**Spirits** - **Liquors**. The 40% alcohol drinks. Not usually drunk in pints!

**Spotted dick** - Not actually a medical complaint, spotted dick is a *suet* pudding with dried fruit and is an excellent *pudding* in winter with custard.

Chuck was shocked that Charles wanted a spotted dick!

**Spring onions** - You call these **salad onions** or **green onions** or even **scallions**.

**Spring roll** - *See pancake roll.*

**Squash** - This is a sweet, fruit and sugar based **drink** for kids. It comes in concentrated form in big bottles that you just add water to. Similar in idea to the frozen limeade-type drinks in the US.

**Starter** - As well as being part of a car (usually coupled with the word "motor") this is what we call the **appetizer** on a menu. The more upmarket restaurants would use the word "entree", the French word for the first course of a meal.

**Steak & kidney pie** - This is another traditional English dish. Kidney is not popular in the US so try it when you visit. It won't kill you, honest!

**Steak & kidney pudding** - This is variation of the traditional pie. On a cold winter evening there is nothing better. It is steak and kidney in a thick, soft, *suet* pastry crust. Absolutely divine.

**Stock cube** - The cheats way to make *gravy* is to use a stock cube. You'd call it a **bouillon cube**. Either way it's cheating!

**Stodge** - Stodge means **heavy food** - a lot like we used to get at school in the old days. These days our schools serve much better food, though we still haven't gone as far as you guys with letting the franchises in.

**Stone** - Don't be surprised if a Brit tells you there is a stone in his peach or prune. That's what we call a **pit**.

**Stuffed** - When you have had enough to eat it is quite acceptable to tell everyone that you are stuffed. It means you are **full**. When I said that at a dinner party in Texas I got some very strange looks - apparently it has other meanings there.

**Suet** - Suet is a fairly dry white **beef fat**. It is rubbed into flour as a base for many *puddings*. Sweet and savoury.

**Sweets** - Either another word for **dessert** or also the **candies** you give to kids. Scary old men in films say "Would you like a sweetie, little girl?".

**Swiss roll** - **Jelly roll** to you chaps.

**Take-away** - This word has several meanings. First it is the place that only sells food to **take out**. You might go to the take-away for an Indian or Chinese. If you got a take-away for dinner it would mean the meal itself. Also if you go to a restaurant where you can choose where you eat it then you would be asked if you want to "eat in or take away". You would say here or **to go**.

**Tart** - If you **flirt** with members of the opposite sex you could be described quite legitimately as a tart. If you are a **pastry base** with jam or fruit topping you would also be a tart. But in this instance you may have cream or custard poured over you!

**Tea** - One of the English classics. Tea is either a drink made from tea leaves (loose in a pre warmed pot), boiling water, served in china cups, milk first and at about 4 o'clock in the afternoon. Or tea is the name for the meal served early evening, nowadays by Grandma and Grandad since most modern folk eat **dinner** at about 7:30pm or later.

**Tin** - We seem to have two words for a **can** of food. You could say a tin of beans or a can of beans and they would mean exactly the same.

**Toad in the hole** - You may see this on the menu in a pub or restaurant. It is basically *Yorkshire pudding* or **batter with sausages** embedded in it. It's not special but it is cheap to make.

**Tomato sauce** - **Ketchup** to you chaps - although we use both names here.

**Treacle pudding** - There's nothing nicer than a hot, steaming treacle pudding on a cold winter night. Smothered in custard and without a single calorie! Well maybe I lied about the last bit. Treacle pudding is a **steamed pudding**, eaten for dessert with a runny *syrup* topping.

**Vacuum flask** - A vacuum flask is a **thermos** to you. It keeps hot things hot and cold things cold. I have an ice cream and some coffee in mine. Not!

**Water** - This is a tricky one. The word is the same in both languages (at least as far as the spelling goes). However, when I asked a waitress for water once, she told me they didn't have any! In Texas you should ask for WAAH DUR! In one embarrassing incident I said to a salesman in a washing machine shop "Is water metered here?".

He said he didn't know and went to see if he worked in different department. When he came back he said there was nobody called Walter Metered working in the shop!

**White** - When someone in the UK asks you how you take your tea or coffee you should say "black", "white without" or "white with". White means **with milk** and the "with" and "without" bit refers to the sugar. I have mine white with one. When I first told a waitress in Texas I wanted my coffee "white with", she said "with what - milk?". Think about it!

**White sauce** - This is called **gravy** in Texas. It is made from flour, butter and milk.

**Wine gums** - These are a kind of *sweet* that are made from the same stuff as Gummi-bears. They are bigger and round and very useful for shutting the kids up for about an hour!

**Yorkshire pudding** - You may see this on the menu in a pub or restaurant. It is a light **batter** that rises when it is cooked. In pubs you will sometimes see huge ones that rise at the edges to form a sort of bowl. The middle can be filled with anything from sausages and beans, to soup or stew. Worth a try if they look good. Traditionally, smaller Yorkshire puds are served with roast beef, as an accompaniment with horseradish sauce and *gravy*, roast spuds and veggies. Quite yummy. Apparently called **pop-overs** in some parts of the US.

# Clothing

Charles was sure Chuck had said pants and suspenders.

**Anorak** - A very untrendy kind of waterproof, padded coat with a zip. The sort of thing your mother made you wear when you were 10 and you still haven't forgiven her for it! Especially if she made you put the hood up when it rained. Possibly called a **slicker** in American. The worst thing about my anorak was that my Mum had tied my gloves together by passing a piece of string through the arms of the anorak. This would have been quite sensible if the big boys hadn't taken great delight in pulling one glove really hard and watching me punch myself in the face with the other hand!

**Balaclava** - This is what you call a **ski mask**. You know - the knitted woollen thing that covers your whole head - with little holes for your eyes, nose and mouth. Not sexy for a first date - but damned useful for robbing banks.

**Boiler suit** - An all-in-one **coverall** that protects clothes from oil and filth in dirty working conditions. Originally used my men working in boiler rooms.

**Boob tube** - One of the more descriptive articles of ladies clothing, the boob tube is an elasticated tube that covers the boobs. In the US some people call the TV a boob tube. Wearing a boob tube would take on a whole new meaning! Watching boob tubes in the UK can get you arrested! I heard them called **tube tops** in the US.

**Brace** - The metal thing you wear on your teeth to make them nicer when you grow up. Not to be confused with ***braces***.

**Braces** - The things you call **suspenders**, our braces hold our *trousers* up.

**Bum bag** - **Fanny pack** in American. Watch the Brits snigger whenever you mention a **fanny pack**! It translates particularly badly - see *fanny*.

**Cagoule** - A thin, windproof jacket. I used to have one that folded up into itself, which was just as well because it was yellow, so the smaller the better in my view. Used in outside pursuits because they take up almost no space when wrapped up. Mentioned in the British TV series, Absolutely Fabulous - yes this is what they are talking about.

**Cardie** - **Cardigan**. Sweater with buttons down the front like a shirt. Very popular with *trainspotters* but nobody else.

**Cozzy** - Grab your cozzy - we're going swimming. It is short for your **swimming costume**, or **bathing suit**.

**Dinner jacket** - **Tuxedo**. We usually refer to it as our DJ. Not to be confused with a Disc Jockey - we definitely don't wear them!

**Dressing gown** - **Robe** to you.

**Dungarees** - **Overalls** to you. Fine on kids but whatever you call them, grown men look ridiculous in them!

**Frock** - This is the word for **dress**, though generally only used by older people. Your posh frock would be your **best dress**.

**Jersey** - As well as being the name of an island near here it is also what we call a **sweater**.

**Jumper** - Another word for **sweater**.

**Knickers** - This is what we call a ladies' **panties**. Not to their face, of course!

**Mac** - Short for **Macintosh**, the Mac is a raincoat invented by a Mr Macintosh. Most likely heard in reference to dirty old men, or flashers, who are stereotyped as wearing macs!

**Muffler** - Don't worry if someone asks you if you would like to wear a muffler. They are not suggesting you wear an old car part round your shoulders. It's actually a big fluffy **scarf**.

Chuck didn't see the point in wearing a muffler.

**Nappy** - **Diaper** to you.

**Pants** - Don't make a comment about an Englishman's pants - they are his **underwear**! Same for ladies too, though *knickers* would be more common. We were in a pub in England one day when two attractive American girls walked in wearing quite short skirts and one loudly said to the other that she was cold and that she should have worn pants! Needless to say she instantly had the attention of every Englishman in the place, who thought there was nothing under her skirt!

**Pinafore** - A pinafore dress is what you might call a **jumper**.

**Pinny** - Mrs Tiggywinkle - the well beloved hedgehog from my childhood, always wore a pinny. Actually childish slang for *pinafore*. You might call it an **apron**, to protect the clothes from washing and cooking. It originates from "pin - afore". In other words you would "pin" it "afore" (in front of) your dress.

**Polo neck** - I can't believe they've come back into fashion - they look so stupid, like you are trying to hide a *love bite*. You call them **turtle necks**.

Charles was sure Chuck had said pants and suspenders.

**Pullover** - Yet another word for **sweater**. Hey it's cold here - we need several names for them!

**Pumps/Plimsolls** - You'd probably call them **sneakers**, but pumps were usually black and elasticated and you wore them during P.E. (Physical Education). They were also called plimsolls as they were invented by the same guy who invented the plimsoll line on ships. These days I'm sure kids wear the latest Nike or Reebok fashion shoes but pumps or plimsolls was what I wore and I was proud of them! By the way, pumps were what one family I used to know, used as the polite word for **farts**. Very strange - who pumped?

**Suspenders** - This one is a bit worrying. Suspenders in English are the things that hold up a lady's (hopefully!) stockings. The first time a male American friend told me he was wearing suspenders to a party I thought it was a Rocky Horror Show party - so I wore suspenders too! Whoops! You call them **garter belts**.

**Swimming costume** - This is what you wear to go swimming, obviously! You might call it a **bathing suit**. We also say swimsuit and *cozzy*.

**Tights** - What you call **pantyhose**! Also a way that kids remember the difference between stalagmites and stalactites. The tights come down and the mites go up!!! Typical of the British education system.

**Trainers** - Short for training shoes. You would call them **sneakers**.

**Trousers** - What you call **pants**! Confused yet? My suspenders friend also told me that he would be wearing **pants** with his *suspenders*. Kinky!

**Vest** - Worn by old men and anyone who is *nesh* (a wimp!), a vest is worn under your shirt to keep you warm. Comes in string vest or plain. You call them **undershirts**.

**Waistcoat** - Worn under your *dinner jacket*, the waistcoat is called a **vest** in America.

**Wellies** - Wellington Boots, named after the Duke of Wellington. Called **galoshes** in America.

# Motoring

Charles was surprised to hear that Chuck drove a stick.

**AA** - The Automobile Association. Similar to your **AAA** these guys come to your car when you breakdown. Unlike the AAA, they carry a workshop with them and fix the car at the side of the street if they can, or carry your car anywhere in the country if they can't. Saved my life a few times. Not to be confused with Alcoholics Anonymous who will come to your car and counsel you on your drinking problem. Make sure you *ring* the right AA!

**Aerial** - **Antenna**. An aerial is on a car, an antenna would be found on insects and aliens from outer space.

**Amber** - Not only do our traffic lights go in a different sequence to yours but we don't have **yellow**! Well actually we do but we always call it amber. The sequence is red, red and amber (together), green. Then green, amber, red. Yours go from red straight to green.

**Articulated lorry** - This is a **trailer truck**. Nothing to do with being well-spoken of course! Usually shortened to artic.

**Banger** - An **old car**. Your first car is usually an old banger. Not to be confused with a kind of sausage!

**Belisha beacon** - These are the orange flashing globes at each side of a *zebra crossing*.

**Bonnet** - Your car's **hood**. Also an old fashioned hat.

**Boot** - Your car's **trunk**. In England, elephants have trunks, not cars!

**Bulb** - When your *indicator* stops working you probably need a new bulb. Don't ask for a **lamp**.

**Bump start** - When you buy your first car as a student in the UK, one of the first lessons you learn is how to bump start it. When the battery is flat you get a couple of strong mates to push you along the street, with the key in the ON position, second gear engaged and your foot on the clutch. When you reach enough speed you take your foot off the clutch, your mates hit their faces on the back of the car and with luck - the car starts! Don't try this in America, it doesn't work with automatics! If you do have a manual car it would be **popping the clutch**.

**Bus station** - The place where the busses start from on their journey. You might call it a **terminal**.

**Cab** - In London you will hear **taxis** referred to as cabs. The London black cab is not only famous for being very distinctive but also for being the first cab to take wheelchairs through the doors.

**Cabriolet** - **Convertible**. As in - why do blondes prefer cabriolets?. Obvious really - more legroom!

**Call** - I remember the announcer at Bristol railway station telling us that the train at platform 10 would call at Nailsea, Backwell, Weston-super-Mare, Highbridge, Bridgwater and Taunton. It would call at the stations, not **stop** at them.

**Car park** - **Parking lot**. Normally uncovered.

**Cat's eyes** - In the middle of British roads there are little white reflectors. They are made of glass and are designed just like the eyes of a cat. They are mounted in a rubber housing and inserted into a hole in the road surface. When a car drives over them, they are pushed into the hole and when they pop back up - they are cleaned! Clever huh? **Road reflectors** are the nearest thing you have in the US. The guy who invented them actually came across a cat facing him on a dark night. Lucky it wasn't facing the other way - or he might have invented the pencil sharpener!!

**Cattle class** - A rather unflattering, but not inaccurate, description of **coach** class air travel!

**Central reservation** - Not where you call for airline tickets or where Indians live. This is the bit of grass or kerbing between the carriageways on a *dual carriageway* or *motorway*. **Median** in American.

**Chunnel** - The famous **channel tunnel** is called the chunnel. If you visit London it is well worth taking the 3 hour train ride from Waterloo, right into the heart of Paris.

**Coach** - We differentiate between a coach and a bus. A bus is usually the sort that you pay as you enter and the routes are not generally that long. They drive through the towns and villages of the UK. A coach normally goes from city to city, more like US **greyhounds**. They have fewer or no stops at all and you would buy a ticket in advance.

**Crash** - Same as a *pile-up* but involving fewer vehicles. Also called a **wreck** in the US.

**Cul-de-sac** - **Dead end** to you. The American expression "dead end" is a bit more to the point really. Cul-de-sac comes from the French.

**De-mister** - **De-froster** in American. Most cars have them on the back window. Some have them on the front too. Very useful during your first date when you borrow your Dad's car! Most Texans would never have a use for either!

**Diversion** - **Detour** in America.

**Double decker** - This is a **bus**. One that has an upstairs and a downstairs. They were abundant when I was using them as a kid but nowadays most of them seem to have ended up as tourist buses around New York and other large US cities. Sometimes with the roof removed. They also have "Genuine London Bus" in huge letters down the side for some reason.

**Double yellow lines** - The double yellow lines are the **no parking zone**. Well I suppose you could park there but the chances are the car won't be there when you return. The *traffic wardens* are pretty hot on cars parked on double yellows. By the way - you can generally park on single yellow lines after 6pm and at weekends unless it says otherwise on a nearby lamp-post.

**Drink driving** - This particular pastime is illegal in both countries. You call it **drunk driving**.

**Drunk in charge** - In the same way that you have **DWI** and **DUI** offences for "driving while intoxicated" and for "driving under the influence", we just have "drunk in charge" (never shortened to DIC for obvious reasons!). All three are best avoided in both countries occifer!

**Dual carriageway** - **Divided highway**. All have a 70mph speed limit unless indicated (posted) otherwise.

**Due care and attention** - This is the name of a motoring offence that covers many driving sins. I got my first ticket on the M4 at about midnight for driving without due care and attention. I was actually driving in the middle lane of the motorway, when I should have been in the inside lane.

**Economy** - When we travel in an aeroplane in the cheap seats we are travelling economy. You would be travelling **coach**. To us - that's a sort of bus, more suited to the roads than 37,000 feet!

**Estate car** - An elongated version of a normal saloon car. Many cars have an estate version. In American the nearest thing is a **station wagon**.

**Excess** - **Deductible**. The amount you pay before your car insurance does. Insurance is one of the few things that is much cheaper in the UK than the USA. My car insurance cost me between 2-4 times as much in Texas as it did in England.

**Fire engine** - What you would call a **fire truck**.

**Flyover** - No, not what happens in Starsky and Hutch, when they drive too fast in San Francisco over bumps - this is an **overpass**.

**Fog lights** - This one took me two years to realise. In America fog lights are white and are at the front of the car, low down. In England they are very intense red and are on the back of the car, so that in real fog, the car behind you can see you. This is important if you are importing a US car to the UK as you have to get this fixed.

**Ford** - If you see a sign saying "ford ahead" in England, it is not warning you that an American car is blocking a country lane. It is actually telling you there is a **low water crossing** ahead.

**Gallon** - This would be **1.25 gallons** to you. Ours are 25% bigger than yours.

**Gas** - A substance used to cook with and to heat homes. Cars do not run on gas, they use *petrol*.

**Gearstick** - The **stick shift**. Most cars in England come with a gearstick. If you learn to drive in one without a gearstick you may not drive one that does until you take the test in that sort too! I thought Texans must have thought I looked like a witch when they asked me if I drove a stick!! What a strange question.

**Give way** - **Yield**. At a roundabout you give way to the right. In Texas, apparently, yielding is optional, more dependent on the size of the vehicles involved.

**Glove box** - This is the little cubby hole in the front of the car where you keep *sweet* wrappers, parking tickets and old chewing gum. A **glove compartment** to you.

**Hand brake** - Your **parking brake**. Some American cars have foot operated ones but in the UK they are generally hand operated only. Since most UK cars are *manual* they are probably more often used in the UK.

**Head lamp** - **Headlight**, though we use either word.

**Hire car** - **Rental car**. When hiring a car in England, remember to specify an automatic or you will get one with a gearstick.

**Hooter** - The hooter is the **horn** on your car. It is also another word for a persons' **nose**. Therefore, if someone steps out in front of you in the UK, be sure to press the right one!

**Indicator** - **Turn lights**. The little orange lights on each corner of your car that tell other road users your intended direction of travel, if not straight on. In England it is illegal for the brake lights to double up as indicators, like they do in the USA. In America use of these lights appears to be optional (unless travelling in a straight line).

**Jam sandwich** - This is a motorway **police car**. It is called a jam sandwich because if it is white with a bright orange stripe along the side, that's just what it looks like. Obviously it is a bit bigger and has wheels and a couple of uniformed gentlemen inside it, but hey!

**Juggernaut** - What you would call an **18 wheeler** - any large *lorry* would be a juggernaut.

**Lay-by** - On the side of the road you will often find a lay-by, probably just a widening of the road without any kerbing, to allow you to stop and take a break. It doesn't quite qualify as a **rest area** as there are generally no facilities.

**Level crossing** - This is what you call a **grade crossing** - where a railway crosses a road.

**Lights** - The little triangular **windows** on some cars.

**Lorry** - **Truck**. Although the chaps that drive them ARE sometimes called truckers. They are usually called lorry drivers and are not allowed to use the fast lane on England's motorways. To add to the confusion I just met a lady in Minnesota called Laurie, which I thought was hilarious, so I call her "truck"!

**Lorry driver** - **Truck driver** or **trucker** to you.

**Manual** - A car in England is either a manual or an automatic (transmission). A manual has a gearstick. You would call them a **stick** or **stick shift**. When we say we drive a manual, you say you drive a **stick**. In England the only people who drive sticks are witches!!

Charles was surprised to hear that Chuck drove a stick.

**Motorway** - **Freeway**. Very strict rules apply to motorways, only drive faster than 100mph if you are happy to lose your licence (or are very good at haggling!). Always drive in the slow lane, unless overtaking (or risk being arrested). Always enter and exit via slip roads on the left hand side.

**Multi-storey** - Short for multi-storey car park. Means a **parking garage** on several levels.

**Near side lane** - The **slow lane** to you, though to us, all your lanes are slow! (Sorry - couldn't resist it!).

**No entry** - I love the "no entry" signs in the US, they are so descriptive. They just say **Wrong way**! No chance of mistaking the meaning there!

**Number plate** - **Licence plate** in the US. In the UK they tell you the age of the vehicle and have some coding to identify the area of the country the car was registered in. The format is G992 CAJ where the first letter tells you the car was registered between Aug 1 199x and July 31st of the following year! The following year will start with an H and so on. The UK makes big business from personalised number plates, just like in the

US, but we need to keep them in the format. Recently I tried to get M1 KEY so that it would look like MIKEY! It was too expensive - shame! Our number plates generally stay with the car, whereas yours seem to stay with the person.

**Overtake** - **Pass** in the US. We can only do it on the right. In Texas they do it in whatever lane they like. Don't try that here - you'll be arrested. Our cops don't have guns but they don't half *take the piss!*

**Pavement** - Pavement in English is **sidewalk** in American. The first chapter in the Texas driving handbook says that you must drive on the pavement at all times! Yikes!

**Pelican crossing** - The black and white bars across the road with a green and red man lighting up to show pedestrians when to walk and when to stay.

**Petrol** - **Gasoline**. Ask for a *petrol station* when you run out. More expensive than the American sort but comes in bigger *gallons*.

**Petrol station** - **Gas station** to you. Prepare to be shocked at the prices!

**Pile-up** - What happens when a number of cars collide into each other. Known as a **wreck** in America.

**Prang** - If you have a prang in your car - it means you have hit a car or another object. Prangs tend be less serious than *write-offs* as they can be fixed.

**RAC** - Royal Automobile Club. Another roadside assistance company, similar to the American **AAA**. They drive mobile garages and can fix most things on the roadside. They will even drive you to the other end of the country if necessary, to get you there!

**Red route** - When driving around London watch out for the roads with yellow lines that are RED! These are special red routes designed to keep the traffic moving and free of obstructions. Park on a red route and the British police will shoot to kill!

**Road works** - If you see a sign with "road works" on it, be careful because it means **men working**.

**Roof** - The **top** of a convertible car is called the roof in England.

**Roof-rack** - This is the **luggage rack** to you.

**Roundabout** - **Traffic circle**. The best bit about arriving in England after a long transatlantic flight with no sleep and finding there are no automatic cars, is that the first obstacle you find at any airport is a big roundabout. They are scary if you have never seen one before. The simple rule is "give way (yield) to the right". In other words, the traffic already on the roundabout has right of way. In Malta, however, the traffic approaching the roundabout has right of way, which is why Brits on holiday in Malta keep killing themselves!

**Saloon** - A non-estate car. You might call it a **sedan**. Saloon is also one of the bars in a traditional pub.

**Second class** - When we travel in the cheap seats of a train or plane, we are travelling second class. You would be travelling **coach**.

**Silencer** - **Muffler**. Or the thing you put on a gun to make killing people quieter.

**Slip road** - **Entry ramp** or **exit ramp**.

**Spanner** - Something to keep in your *boot* - a **wrench**.

**Subway** - This is the tunnel that allows pedestrians to walk under a busy road. You would call it an **underpass**.

**Tailback** - To see a proper tailback in England - join the M25 at any point on a Friday evening. It means **bumper to bumper** but on the M25 there is no start or finish - it goes right round London. That's why they call it the London orbital car park.

**Tick over** - If you leave your car ticking over, it would be **idling** in the US.

**Ton** - I remember telling my friends at the office that I was stopped doing a "ton twenty" up the M40 at the weekend. We use the word ton to mean **one hundred miles an hour**. Clearly a "ton twenty" is a hundred and twenty miles and hour. It's a long story but he even let me off! Lucky huh?

**Traffic wardens** - We never came across traffic wardens in Texas. The nearest thing we saw was the **traffic cops**. Our wardens wander the streets of our towns in their black uniforms, hiding until you leave your car illegally parked for 1 or 2 nano-seconds then they write you a ticket and stick it your screen before you can say "You B****rd".

**Transporter** - I think these are referred to as **car carriers** in the US. They are the huge *lorries* that carry up to 10 cars in precarious positions.

**Turn right** - **Make a turn**. We don't "make" turns in the UK, we just turn. So when you'd make a left at the light, we would turn left at the light.

**Verge** - The **grassy edge** to a road. You park on the verge if you break down to avoid being hit by the traffic.

**Windscreen** - The English word for **windshield**.

**Windscreen wipers** - The English for **windshield wipers**.

**Wing** - **Fender** to you. To us a fender is a kind of guitar!

**Write-off** - This is when you have **wreck**ed your car. Or **totalled** it. It comes from the fact that the insurance companies have calculated that it would cost more to repair the car than to replace it. So the value is written off the books.

**Zebra crossing** - Similar to the *pelican* but with flashing orange beacons on either side. If a pedestrian steps onto a *pelican crossing*, you should stop. Unless you are in London in which case your job is to kill them.

Chuck just couldn't see a zebra crossing.

It wasn't the noses that caught Charles' eye!

**Anorak** - No, not an article of clothing in this instance. An anorak is another word for a **nerd** or a **square**. Apparently originated from the anoraks that were worn by *trainspotters* whatever the weather. If you are described as being a bit of an anorak, beware!

**Barmaid** - A female **bartender** in a pub is called the barmaid.

**Barman** - The **bartender** in a pub is called the barman.

**Barrister** - An **attorney** that would represent you in court. Not that I know, of course!

**Beefeater** - This is the name given to the **guards** at the Tower of London and a chain of cheap steak restaurants. One is worth visiting, one is worth avoiding!

**Bender** - A bender is a **gay man**. Also referred to as a *woofter* and a few rather unsavoury terms that you'll have to visit England to find out!

**Berk** - A **fool**. I remember giggling every time James Burke came on telly when I was kid. Also spelt "burk". The origin is quite interesting - it is another rhyming slang word that many people don't even realise is short for "Berkeley-Hunt", who was an 1890s stage idiot. Hunt rhymes with, well use your imagination! It's OK to say berk.

**Big girl's blouse** - This is a nice way of saying someone is a **wimp**. It means someone is being **pathetic**. It works well for girls and blokes.

**The Bill** - The **police**, or the thing you ask for after a meal in a restaurant. In the US that is called the **check**.

**Bird** - Your bird is your **girl**. A bit old fashioned and only used by your Dad or Grandad. Not very politically correct.

**Bloke** - A **guy** in American. A good bloke would be like a **nice guy**.

**Bobby** - Yet another word for **policeman**.

**Boffin** - This is the word for a **nerd**. Usually male, a boffin would be highly intelligent, have no dress sense and probably grow up to be a mad scientist or an HTML programmer!

**Bonce** - Your bonce is your **head**! So if someone tells you to use your bonce it means "think about it".

**Bristols** - This is a good example of a word that most Brits would know, but not necessarily realise it was derived from rhyming slang. Bristols means **breasts**. If you haven't worked it out yet, bristols is short for bristol city's (a football team), city's rhymes with titties, i.e. breasts! Easy huh!

**Brum** - Short for **Birmingham**. People from brum are brummies and they speak brum, a kind of English!

**Brummy** - A person from Birmingham who speaks *brum*.

**Bum chum** - Another name for a **gay man**. We have lots of other expressions, too numerous to list here. Some of the less offensive include shirtlifter and *arse* bandit.

**Buns** - Some elderly ladies have buns on their heads. This is not a terrible deformity, the bun is actually rolled up hair in the shape of a currant bun.

**Burk** - **Fool**. I remember giggling every time James Burke came on telly when I was kid. Also spelt *berk*.

**Busker** - **Street entertainer** to you. Someone who makes his or her living by singing, playing or acting on the street to amuse the crowds of passers by. Busking is down to a fine art at Covent Garden in London - it's worth the trip. Reminds me of the buskers outside Quincey Market in Boston.

**Butterfingers** - You would call someone butterfingers if they were **clumsy** and dropped something.

**Cack-handed** - Someone who is cack-handed is **clumsy**. My Mum was putting her buns in the oven one afternoon and tipped the tray upside down and said she was all cack-handed.

**Cake hole** - This is another one I heard a lot as a kid. My Dad use to say "Shut your clanging cake hole". Now that I am a foot taller than him he might say something more like "Could you please be quiet"! It basically means your **mouth**.

**Cashier** - This is the person in the bank who talks to the public over the counter. You would call them **tellers**.

**Chalk and cheese** - This isn't some weird British recipe, it is short for the expression "as different as chalk and cheese". You hear it when people are bitching about other couples they know who are very different to each other. You might say like **night and day**.

**Chap** - A **guy** in American. Men and women are sometimes referred to as chaps and chapesses.

**Christian name** - This is your **first name**. You would see it on forms that require both parts of your name separately. We generally ignore middle initials as fairly irrelevant and avoid the use of additions like "junior" and "IIIrd", unless you happen to be a king, of course.

**Chuck** - Another term of endearment from up north. Pronounced more like chook. Rhymes with dook!

**Chum** - Your chum is your **friend**. We might also say *mate*.

**Clever clogs** - Same as *clever dick* and *smart arse* - this is a **wise guy**.

**Clever dick** - This is a bit of a **wise guy**, not performing tricks with certain parts of the body!

**Clot** - If someone calls you a clot, please be offended. It means you are stupid. *A dim wit*! Of course, if you really are a clot, then you probably won't notice!

**Cloth ears** - This is the polite way to call someone a deaf *git*. Politely put it simply means you are **deaf**.

**Codger** - An old codger is an old *bloke*. An **old timer** to you.

**Copper** - Either a **policeman** or the **coins** in your pocket that are not silver.

**Dapper** - If you are particularly **well dressed**, you would be described as being dapper.

**Dim wit** - Someone who is **thick** is a dim wit or just dim. Avoid using this word when addressing police in the UK, but feel free to try it in the US!

**Dip stick** - Apart from being something you find in your car, a dip stick is someone who is **stupid** or who has done something stupid. I get called it all the time!

**Divvy** - This is another word like *dip stick* for someone who is a bit **stupid**.

**Dog's body** - A dog's body is a **gofer**. Someone who gets all the menial tasks to do, like fetching and carrying. It doesn't mean they have four legs and a tail.

**Don** - I recently took a friend from Austin to Oxford to punt up the river and have a cream tea in the university. We ate in the main hall of one of the colleges and at one end there is separate table for the dons. They are the **professors** at Oxford or Cambridge universities.

**Duck** - Another term of endearment from up north. Pronounced more like "dook". Rhymes with "chook"!

**Duffer** - An old duffer is either someone who is not very good at something or someone who is old. Like an **old geezer**.

**Dustman** - The man who empties your dustbin. **garbage collector** in the US.

**Estate agents** - The people who can make even the most disgusting property sound desirable - **realtors** to you.

**Father Christmas** - **Santa Claus** in America, though I'm not sure he's the same bloke. I saw him in London when I was leaving for New York, and when I arrived, hey he was there too!

**Fire brigade** - This is the **fire department**. Dial 999 for a demonstration.

**Flat mate** - This is what you call a **room mate**. It's someone you share your *flat* with. After all the clue is in the name. Whenever an American tells me they have a room mate I worry about them sharing a room at their age - or even question their sexuality!

**Flower** - Whenever I visit my relatives up north I seem to be called "flower" quite often. It is simply a term of endearment. I reckon they call you that when they can't remember your real name!

**Forehead** - Actually this is the same word in both languages. It is just the pronunciation that is different. Generally in the US it is pronounced fore-head and in the UK it is forrid.

**Fresher** - During your first year at university you would be referred to as a fresher. You would be called a **freshman** in the US.

**Gaffer** - This is a word for an old *bloke* or a workman's **boss** or the **foreman** of a team of labourers. A good gaffer would be a good boss.

**Geezer** - Another word for *bloke* but mostly heard in London.

**Git** - I have never been able to describe this northern term for someone who is a **jerk**, an undesirable, a *prat*. "You ignorant git" is a popular use of the word.

**Gob** - This word is used as a noun, meaning your **mouth**, hence the gobstopper is used to fill it up! The other use is as a verb. You would not gob your gobstopper out as it would be rude. Some people gob on the pavement, meaning they **spit** green stuff out in public. Not nice.

**Gooseberry** - To be a gooseberry is to be the **third person on a date**. If two guys are in bar and one of them successfully chats up a girly, his mate becomes a gooseberry and feels a bit awkward! You would feel a bit of a gooseberry if you accompanied a couple on a date.

**Grockles** - This is a word I heard a lot when I was a kid in the West Country. It means **tourists**. So if you hear someone in the UK mention the word "grockles" they are probably talking about you!

**Guard** - When travelling by train, the man that collects your tickets is called a guard, not a **conductor** as you have in the US. Strangely if it was a bus we would call them a conductor, even though they don't have a baton and there is no orchestra in sight!

**Gumby** - This is mild insult that is safe to use in public when someone is not using their brain. Used with people you know usually, though you could try calling your British waiter a gumby when he brings you water with no ice in it - see where the water ends up!

**Guv** - I've been called "Guv" or "Guv'nor" a few times by taxi drivers in London. It's an East End expression, short for "Governor" which roughly translates as **Sir**, used to address a man when you don't know his name.

**Hooray Henry** - I am not aware of an American equivalent to a hooray henry. It is a phrase that came in a few years ago to describe the young upper class. They talk like they have a plum in their mouths and say things like "OK yar"! Similar to **yuppie**.

It wasn't the noses that caught Charles' eye!

**Hooter** - Your hooter is your **nose**. The clue is in the noise you make when you blow it! Some people even have one that looks like a hooter, just for effect I think. It's also the **horn** on a car. Just imagine how shocked Brits must be when they go to the bar you have called Hooters and they find that the waitresses all have normal noses - disappointing!

**Jammy beggar** - You may hear people being called a jammy bugger, jammy beggar or jammy bastard. It just means they have been **lucky**!

**Job's worth** - A job's worth is a person who is inflexible in their job, even if it means upsetting their customer. For example, if a restaurant served custard with apple pie and you wanted ice cream instead, a job's worth would be the kind of waiter who would refuse to give you ice cream because it wasn't listed like that on the menu. The excuse would be that it was more than their job's worth.

**Konk** - This is not a very nice way of describing someone's **nose**.

**Landlady** - The lady owner (or these days more often the manager) of a *pub* is called the landlady. Stems from the origin of most pubs being inns with accommodation. Many still do of course, though the name landlady applies to all pub owners, even if they have no rooms to let.

**Landlord** - The same as *landlady* except where the proprietor is a *bloke*!

**Loaf** - My Dad was always telling me to use my loaf. It means use your **head** and comes from rhyming slang. Loaf is short for loaf of bread, which rhymes with **head**.

**Lollipop man** - Every kid loves the lollipop man (or lady of course). They stand in the middle of the street and hold this huge lollipop up to stop the traffic as the kids cross the road. Actually it's not a real lollipop - it is a sign that tells the traffic to "STOP, CHILDREN CROSSING". Sometimes called a **crossing guard** in the US.

**Long sighted** - We say long sighted when you would say **far sighted**.

**Lug holes** - These are your **ears**.

**Mate** - **Buddy** or **friend**. You might go to the *pub* with your *mates* for a few *lagers* followed by a greasy *doner*.

**Mean** - We often say people are mean if they are **tight fisted**, **stingy** or hold on to their money. This often confuses my American chums who think I'm talking about people being horrid.

**Morris dancer** - Around May, you are likely to see a group of morris dancers, seemingly sane men who dress up in knee length britches, long socks, with ribbons flying from various parts of their bodies. They dance around poles with long sticks in their hands much to the amusement of passers by. Then they go home and don't come out until the following May.

**Mother** - Don't be alarmed if a British bloke says "Shall I be Mother?". This would happen when the family sit down to a pot of tea or a slice of cake and someone needs to pour or cut for everyone. Whoever gets to do the honours is being "Mother".

**Mum** - **Mom** in the US.

**Namby pamby** - Avoid being called a namby pamby when visiting the UK. It means you are acting like a *big girl's blouse*! You're being a **wimp** - like not having the courage to try *haggis* or *black pudding*.

**Naughty bits** - If you have seen the British TV show, Monty Python, you may have come across this rather silly expression for describing ones **genitals**.

**Nobby no-mates** - An imaginary name for someone with **no friends**. You call people this when they have not been invited to something you have, just to be horrid!

**Nosey parker** - Someone who sticks their nose into everyone elses business.

**Nutter** - Someone who is **crazy** would be described as a nutter - you might say a **nutcase**.

**On your tod** - If you are on your tod it means you are all **on your own**. A more recent expression is to say you were *Nobby no-mates*. Ahh, sad!

**Page three girl** - One of the cheap and cheerful newspapers in the UK is The Sun. It is most famous for it's page three girl, a different topless girl every day. Of course, most people buy it for the news. Mmmm!

**Pillock** - Another mildly insulting name for someone. If someone had just done something stupid you would say "you pillock". This one is safe in front of grandparents.

**Plod** - The **police**. This one originates from an Enid Blyton character in the Noddy stories - Mr Plod the Policeman. I hope the Teletubbies don't make their way into the English language in the same way - just imagine - "I'm off to clean the carpet with the Noo Noo" or "I'm out of the closet now everyone knows I'm a Tinky Winky".

**Plonker** - Either another word for your **penis**, your *John Thomas* or your dick. Or an inoffensive term for someone who is a bit of a *wally*. Most well known in the phrase "Rodney - you plonker" from the British sitcom, Only Fools and Horses. If someone is *taking the piss*, or making fun of you, they would also be pulling your plonker.

**Po-faced** - When we were kids, if someone told a rude joke at the dinner table and everyone laughed - sometimes my Dad would sit there po-faced. In other words he was not amused and would keep a **straight face**. Actually he would remember the joke for work but wasn't going to admit that to the kids was he now!! Probably derived from "poker faced".

**Ponce** - Poncey things and poncey people are a bit girlie! It is not exactly another word for **gay** but it's getting close. A ponce is also another word for **pimp**, who lives off a prostitute's earnings. And it also has another meaning and that is to **scrounge** so one might try to ponce a *fag* off your *mate*, meaning you would **scrounge a cigarette**.

**Poofter** - An extended version of the word "poof", this is how you could refer either to a **gay man** or to a guy who is being a bit of a *nancy boy* or *woofter*.

**Posty** - Your postman is the posty. You would call him the **mailman**.

**Prefect** - I hated the prefects at school. They are your peer students who are allowed to stay in at lunch times and guard the doors to keep the rest of us out in the cold and the rain - and that was just the summers! You might call them **monitors** though I'm not sure there is a direct translation.

**Punter** - Punters are **customers**. Originally came from the **betters** at the racetracks but has extended in use to mean anyone who should be persuaded to part with their money.

**Randy** - A friend of mine visited a company in the US and was asked to wait in the *reception* with a *cuppa* whilst the receptionist went to "get Randy". My friend said he was just hoping for a biscuit! Randy is not a name in England. It means you're **horny** or you're ready for sex. If your name is Randy, try alternative approaches with Brits!

**Red Indian** - This is an Indian from America. You just call them **Indians**. We use the word "Indians" to mean people from India! Well the clue is in the name!

**Room mate** - This is someone you share your bedroom with in a *flat*. We think you all share rooms because you use this expression to mean someone you share the whole flat with - get it right!

**Scatty** - I know lots of scatty people. Otherwise known as scatterbrains. You would probably call them **whacky** but probably not whackerbrains!

**School leaver** - This is what we call a **college graduate**. Next stop - work or university.

**Scouse** - This is the language used by Liverpudlians (people from Liverpool, like me!). It is basically English but hard to understand. Rhymes with "house".

**Scouser** - Someone from Liverpool would be a scouser.

**Scrubber** - This is a nasty way of referring to a **loose woman**. Similar to *tart* or *floozy*.

**Septic** - Try not to be offended, but this means an **American**. It's actually the rhyming slang for **yank**. Septic is short for "septic tank" and tank rhymes with yank. Now you know!

**Shareholder** - Someone who owns shares in a company. You would call them **stockholders**.

**Short sighted** - We say short sighted when you would say **near sighted**.

**Sideboards** - **Sideburns** in the USA - though we say both words here.

**Skiver** - A skiver is someone who evades something. For example a truant is someone who skives off school instead of studying - I should know!

**Slag** - A slag or an "old slag" is not a very nice way of describing a woman who is a bit loose, a bit of a *slapper*.

**Slapper** - A less offensive word than *slag*, this is another way of calling someone a *tart*, a major **flirt**.

**Smart arse** - No - not a clever bottom, this is someone who is a bit too clever for their own good. A **wise guy**. Often used to describe someone who has an answer for everything.

**Solicitor** - This is our word for an **attorney**. So when we see signs in the US that say "No Soliciting" it sounds like attorneys are not welcome there. Well where are they welcome exactly?

**Sponger** - Someone who borrows or begs and does nothing to earn their own money. People sponge off their friends or some who refuse to work and collect dole money sponge off the state.

**Spotty youth** - This is a generic term used by older people to refer to **teenagers**. The "spotty" refers to the fact that they may well have acne.

**Sprog** - A **baby**. Most people have between 2 and 3 sprogs in the UK. Except the Catholics who have lots!

**Squire** - "Morning squire" is something you may hear in England. Squire is used to mean **Sir**.

**Staff** - We use this word to refer to the **employees** in a company in general.

**Swot** - We used to call the boys at school "girlie swots" if they preferred to do homework and study, rather than proper kids things like shoplifting and hiding from teachers. It was not cool to be a swot. Funny how they all ended up with the best jobs though - must be a coincidence!

**Tart** - You old tart! That's what you'd say to someone whose morals are a little loose. A bit too much **flirting**. Normally you'd hear people being described as having been a tart after the office Christmas party, if they were caught snogging their secretary! People may also dress like a tart - maybe if their skirt is too short! Used to apply only to women but these days it is a mild insult used for both sexes.

Chuck couldn't wait to try a British tart.

**Thick** - If someone is thick it means they are **stupid**. You might hear it said that someone is "thick as shi*" - that means they are **really stupid**! Thicko is a nicer way of saying someone is stupid though - try it on your friends!

**Toff** - A toff is someone who is rather well spoken, **upper class** and looks down on the rest of us. My mate calls them "posh gits".

**Trainspotter** - Not your mate. Not that you'd admit to anyway. A trainspotter is a particularly sad breed of middle-aged man, usually wearing a *cardie* and an *anorak*. He stands on the end of railway station platforms and writes down the registration numbers of trains. Fun eh? Pretty close to a **nerd** in American.

**Tramp** - This is a **homeless person** who begs on street corners. We don't use this word in the flirting sense that you have.

**Turf accountant** - This is one of the words we use to describe a bookie. You will see it outside their shops. We also use the expression **betting shop**. The best place to bet, though, is on the racecourse - great fun.

**Ulcer** - When I got an ulcer in Austin I went to about 5 drug stores before I found someone who had a clue what an ulcer might be. After speaking to all the pharmacists it was the *spotty faced youth* stacking the shelves in Albertson's who told me what I had was a **canker**.

**Up the duff** - If a woman is up the duff it means she is **pregnant**.

**Very well** - When someone says hello to you in England and asks how you are, please don't say **good**. Say you are "very well". Good is a behavioural thing, which would mean you are a good boy or girl and haven't been naughty today!! Which doesn't really answer the question, does it?

**Vet** - In England, vets look after the health of our animals and pets. They are rarely seen loitering on street corners, begging for work or money. The first American who told me he was a vet heard all about my dog before he put me straight! Whoops! You call them **veterinarians** I believe.

Charles decided not to take his dog to the vet after all.

**Wally** - This is another term for someone who has been a bit **stupid**. Unlike the previous examples, this one is safe with the elderly or the young.

**Wazzock** - The same as a *pillock* - it's someone who has done something **stupid**. Not too offensive.

**Weed** - Every school has their fair share of weeds. They are the skinny little **wimps** that wear glasses and get picked on. A healthy part of growing up, I'm sure.

**Woofter** - If you are a **gay** man you might be called a "woolly woofter" or just woofter. This is one of the less offensive terms.

**Wuss** - Pronounced "woos" this is another word for a *big girl's blouse*, or *namby pamby*.

**Yank** - An **American**. The Brits refer to the Americans as yanks in general. Whether you are from the north or the south!

**You lot** - **You guys**. My Dad would often come and find my brothers and I up to no good. He would say "what are you lot up to"?

# Around the house

Chuck waited for Charles to join him in the garden.

**Action replay** - During the world cup the England team scored so few goals we had to watch each one several more times on the action replay. Probably as many times as you watched the USA team on **instant replays**.

**Aga** - A type of **stove** that not only cooks the dinner but in many cases, heats the water and the house too. You used to find an Aga in most farmhouses but they have become a status symbol in the UK and have become very popular in any sort of house.

**Airing cupboard** - In British houses we have a hot water tank in a cupboard off the landing or in one of the bedrooms. Since it is warm in there, we usually hang clothes in it to let them air. That's why we call it the airing cupboard. In my house in Texas, the hot water tank was in the garage.

**Answerphone** - We like to refer to our **answering machines** as answerphones.

**Bathroom** - Again, the clue is in the name. In a British house, you will find a bath in the bathroom. (In smaller houses there may also be a toilet). So when we are going to the bathroom - we are not answering a call of nature - we're going for a bath! Always causes problems when Americans visit UK families this one - I'm sure they think we wee in the sink!

Chuck couldn't find the john in the bathroom.

**Beading** - This is the stuff that goes around the edge of cheap furniture. **Wood trim** to you chaps.

**Bedsit** - This is the kind of accommodation many students live in when they cannot afford anything else. It is basically a single room with a bed, *cooker*, table and sofa. You would normally share the bathroom. The nearest thing you have in the US is an **efficiency**.

**Bin** - **Trash can**. You would put a *bin liner* in it before you put the *rubbish* in it to keep it clean. *Bin day* is the day that the *bin men* in the *bin lorry* come and empty your *dustbin*. A bin would normally mean the one in your house - whereas the *dustbin* would normally mean the one outside - though that sometimes gets called the bin too.

**Bin bag** - The black bag that you put inside the kitchen *bin* to save you having to wash out the *bin* each time you empty it. Often comes with a draw string so that you can tie the top shut and avoid nasty niffs when you put it in the *dustbin*.

**Bin day** - For some reason - everywhere I have lived in the world, bin day is on Monday. I'm sure somewhere it happens on another day but not anywhere I've been!

**Bin liner** - This is another word for *bin bag*.

**Bin lorry** - The vehicle that the *bin men* drive.

**Bin men** - The chaps that come around at 6am and wake the entire street up with their *bin lorry* to empty your *dustbins*. Sometimes the *rubbish* even goes in the *lorry*! I'm sure they have some kind of machine that singles out the *crisp* bags and deposits them along the street!

**Blower** - The blower is the **telephone**, before you get too excited!

**Bog** - A vulgar word for the **toilet**, either the room or the pan itself.

**Box** - If you hear a Brit complaining that there is nothing on the box, he would be talking about the lack of viewing pleasures on the **television**.

**Brolly** - Short for **umbrella**. An essential item in England!

**Budgie** - One of the most popular pets in the UK, a budgie is a small green bird. Budgie is short for budgerigar, which is a small Australian **parakeet**.

Generally they get eaten by the cat or when you let them out, they find the only open window in the house and let themselves out!

**Bungalow** - A house with no upstairs. A **single storey house**. Not popular with anyone but the old.

**Caravan** - Everyone in the UK hates caravans - except caravan owners, that is. They are the **trailer houses** that come out every summer and block all our little British roads and bring everyone to a complete standstill. Aaaaaargggggg!

**Ceefax** - This is the text service found on the TV. On British TVs each channel has a text service as an alternative to the regular programming. You can hit the mute and press the TEXT button and read several hundred pages of info from TV listings to news, from the lottery results to cheap *holiday* deals. Ceefax is the BBC version. On the commercial channels, the equivalent is *teletext*.

**Continental quilt** - This is what we used to call *duvets*. Since the UK was the last country in Europe to figure out what they were, we seem to have made up a name for them. Now we just call them *duvets*.

**Cooker** - The thing in your kitchen that you use to cook things on or in. The top is the *hob* and the inside is the oven. You refer to it as a **range** or **stove**.

**Corn dolly** - On the top of some *thatched* houses there is a model of an animal - often a pheasant. These are made of straw (the same as the roof) and are just there for decoration. Keep a look out for them as you drive around the English countryside.

**Couch** - **Sofa** to you. America has some of the largest furniture in the world, yet the only sofa too small to make love in, you call a love seat!

**Council estate** - A council estate is a neighbourhood of *council houses*.

**Council house** - A council house is a government built house to help people on lower incomes have a home. They all used to be rented from the government but now most tenants have the option to buy relatively cheaply to help them get on the house ownership ladder. Most council houses are fairly large, for families, but not terribly attractive. Called **projects** in some places in the USA.

**Cubby hole** - A cubby hole is a **small nook or cranny**. It originated as a word for the glove box in a car but is now less fussy about its use.

**Cupboard** - Any **closet** in the house. Cupboards in the kitchen contain food, crockery, *cutlery* etc. In the bedroom they contain clothes and sometimes skeletons.

**Des res** - If someone lives in a particularly nice property in a nice part of town it would be referred to as a des res. It is short for **desirable residence** and usually means *bloody* expensive!

**Dresser** - **Dresser hutch** or **china cabinet** seem to be the closest US words for this item of furniture which lives in the kitchen or dining room. The bottom half is an enclosed cabinet and the top is an open, doorless cabinet for standing plates in upright.

**Dust cart** - Another word for the *lorry* that the *bin men* drive.

**Dustbin** - When you empty your bins the day before *bin day*, you put them in the dustbin outside. **Trash can** to you.

**Duvet** - Most Brits have dispensed with blankets and sheets and now sleep under a duvet. It is similar to a **comforter** but has a removable cover that can be washed. Duvet's warmth is measured in togs, 2 or 3 togs for summer duvets and 11 or more for winter ones.

**Earth** - This, in electrical terms is what you call **ground**. You will find appliances that say "this appliance must be earthed"' for example. Or when wiring an electrical plug the third pin will be marked "earth".

**Eiderdown** - Before Brits started to sleep under *duvets*, they would cover their sheets and blankets with an eiderdown. Similar to a **comforter** it does not have a removable cover and is just there to add extra warmth and to look nice.

**Emulsion** - Our paint for the inside of houses is basically split into emulsion and gloss varieties. Emulsion for the walls and gloss for the woodwork and metal surfaces. Emulsions are water based and can come in matt or silk flavours, depending on whether you want a shine or not.

**En-suite** - If you are looking at bed & breakfast listings in the UK you might see reference to an en-suite. This is the **bathroom** and means that it is connected directly to the bedroom and therefore not shared.

**Estate** - This is short for a housing estate. You might call it a **residential development** or a **subdivision**. Basically it is a bunch of similar houses built far too close together and described as "highly desirable" by *estate agents*!

**Flat** - This is our word for an **apartment**. I met someone in Texas who had broken down in his car and he told me that he had a flat. I thought it was a strange time to tell me where he lived!

**Flex** - Although this is derived from the word "flexible", it is used as a noun to mean an **electric cord** or **extension lead**.

**Garden** - Not the vegetable patch or the flower beds. The garden is the **yard**. I always wondered why my American friends thought it was odd that Brits spend so much time sitting in the garden!

Chuck waited for Charles to join him in the garden.

**Gazumping** - When you buy a new house in the UK, you hope that you won't be gazumped. Gazumping is frowned on but it still goes on. When you make an offer on a house and the seller accepts it, they are not allowed to then accept a higher offer from another potential buyer. That would be gazumping.

**Hand basin** - This is another word for a **sink**. Usually refers to the kind found in bedrooms in some older houses. They are intended for washing your hands and face, rather than the dishes.

**Hessian** - This material is what they make sacks from and use on the back of carpets. I believe you call it **burlap**.

**Hob** - The bit on the top of the cooker is called the hob. You call it the **burner**.

**Housing estate** - This is what you'd call a **subdivision**.

**Khazi** - Another word for the *toilet*, generally used by older people.

**Kitchen towel** - **Paper towel** to you chaps.

**Laundry basket** - Where you chuck your smelly clothes when you take them off and before you wash them. **Laundry hamper** to you. To us that would imply a thing full of food, not smelly underwear. Surprise!

**Loft** - Our loft is your **attic**.

**Loo** - Either the **toilet** or the **bathroom**. The most common way to ask for the restroom in an English restaurant would to ask where the loo is. Try it - it works. More old ladies die whilst sitting on the loo than you would think. Official statistic. I know two that did!

**Lounge** - Our **living room** is called the lounge. We also say living room sometimes but lounge is probably more common.

**Mobile home** - **Trailer home**. These are not as common in England as they are in the US. I was shocked when I saw my first trailer home driving down I35 on the back of a *lorry*. I've heard of moving house but that is ridiculous. Of course we cannot use the term "trailer trash" since "mobile home rubbish" doesn't have the same ring about it!

**Paper knife** - A **letter opener**. Also used in murder mysteries to kill people, of course.

**Paraffin** - You call this **kerosene**. Equally a paraffin lamp would be one of those old fashioned lamps with paraffin in the base and a wick which is really hard to light. We still have them, but only when you go on scout camp!

**Plaster board** - **Sheet rock** in Texas. In the UK, plasterboard is used to make ceilings and is also used to make internal walls, it is then covered in a thin layer of real plaster, except in cheap modern houses. In Texas, entire houses are made from sheet rock, which is a bit worrying if it is windy or rainy! If the three little pigs had lived in Texas, they would have been eaten! In some states it's called plaster board, like it is here in the UK and others it's called **drywall**.

**Power point** - This would be an **electric socket** in the US. Ours have three pins, not two. The big one is *earth* and also serves to open the little doors where the other two pins go. This keeps little fingers out, in theory!

**Run the bath** - This means to **fill the tub**. Obviously you have to run the bath before you get in it.

**Sand pit** - Every parent buys a sand pit for the kids to play in and the cat to pee in. **Sand boxes** to you, now available with lids to keep the cat out!

**Schooner** - This is a rather ridiculous looking **sherry glass**, for what the pubs call a "large" sherry. It is not the same as the American glass of the same name.

**Secateurs** - You use a pair of secateurs to cut the shrubs in the *garden* down or to trim bushes. You would call them **hedge clippers** or **pruning shears**. I recently discovered that they use something like secateurs during a caesarean birth to cut your wife open. Not the most pleasant experience!

**Settee** - **Sofa** to you. Whether a small love seat or a big three seater.

**Shammy** - I think you call these **wash leathers**. They are the completely useless cloths, originally made from the skin of the chamois - a wild antelope, the size of a goat. They dry rigid and leave horrible streaks across the windows they are supposed to clean!

**Skirting board** - This is the wood that goes around the bottom of the wall and usually has bits of carpet fluff stuck to it where people were too impatient to wait for the paint to dry before laying the carpet! You chaps call it **baseboard**.

**Tap** - **Faucet**. There will be some on the sink in the *loo*!

**Teletext** - Whenever American friends come to visit us in England they are always fascinated by teletext. On our TVs, text is transmitted along with the programmes. You just press a button from any channel and you get the text channel. There you can book *holidays*, check the lottery results, read the news, check the weather and a hundred other things. And best of all - it's free.

**Telly** - The good old **television**. Still only four channels (actually there are FIVE now. Yikes!). Still no commercials on two of them, still very few commercials on the other two. British television was one of the things I missed most when I lived in Texas.

**Thatch** - There are still many houses in England that have thatch for their roof material. It is basically straw and is very picturesque. Amazingly it keeps the rain out pretty well, but is often covered in a fine wire mesh to keep the birds and mice out since they like it too.

**To let** - You'll see signs around England with "To Let" on them, outside properties. This is the same as **to rent** in the US. Kids love to add a letter "I" in between the two words to make "toilet".

**Toilet** - The Brits are not so shy about their use of the word toilet. In fact, it is perfectly reasonable to ask for the toilet in the most classy of establishments. Our first American visitor asked for the **bathroom**, shortly to return complaining there was no toilet there. Of course there wasn't! That is in the toilet! For some reason, you also call it a **restroom** though I have never seen anyone resting in one yet!

**Trunk call** - This is the old expression for a **long distance call**.

**Video** - We use this word to mean the video cassette recorder or **VCR** to you, as well as the video you put in it. Just like in the US - most people have no idea how to operate it. Only the under 10s have mastered most videos.

**Wardrobe** - Wardrobes are usually free standing wooden *cupboards*, designed for holding clothes on hangers. In America you have **closets**. A walk-in wardrobe is a **walk-in closet**.

**White goods** - When you visit a British store that sells things for the home you will find a section for white goods. These are the electrical **appliances** that you have in your kitchen or utility room like fridges, freezers, washing machines and driers. The name is cunningly derived from their colour!

**Wireless** - This is an old word for a **radio**. See if you can guess where the name came from!

Chuck wondered what other colours were available.

# Odds & sods

Charles casually asks if he can bum a fag.

**24 hour clock** - 24 hour clock is used quite widely in the UK. **Military time**, as you call it, ensures there is no confusion between am and pm times, particularly on timetables for planes and trains for example.

**999** - **911** to you. I have no idea why we have different emergency service numbers. Just to ensure that foreigners never get help when they REALLY need it I guess!

**A-Level** - At 18, school kids take around three A-Levels. These are the qualifications that will get them into university or not, depending on the results. University entrance in the UK is based solely on merit so these exams are important. Similar to **SATs** in the US.

**Advert** - **Commercial**. An advert on the TV (or ad, or advertisement) is what you would call a commercial. We also use the same word for printed ads in magazines and newspapers etc.

**Aeroplane** - **Airplane** to you.

**AGM** - Most clubs, societies and companies hold an Annual General Meeting. In the business sense it is a **meeting of the shareholders**.

**Aluminium** - **Aluminum** to you. Dunno why they are spelt and pronounced differently. It is pronounced Al-u-min-i-um. Maybe it is to differentiate it from Plat-in-i-um. Just kidding!

**American football** - What you call **football**. Now we have it too, we have to give it another name, hence American Football.

**Autocue** - I was involved in making a short training film whilst I was in Austin. I realised autocue was not an American word when I asked for one. Everyone just looked at each other then laughed at me. They had no idea I was asking for a **teleprompter**.

**Autumn** - The season after summer. **Fall** is something we do when we get *pissed*!

**B&B** - All over England and the rest of the UK you will see signs outside people's houses with B&B on them. These are **bed & breakfasts** and are the cheapest kind of accommodation available here. Quite the opposite of American B&Bs as I found out in California. I was amazed to find that the house had been done out like a Laura Ashley shop and cost the earth to stay at. In the UK B&B

basically consists of a room in someone's house and a good cooked breakfast. Don't forget the black pudding!

**Bank holiday** - There are about five bank holidays every year in *Blighty*. They are the days that everyone has off. They are called bank holidays because the banks close on them, as do most businesses. In America they are called **public holidays**. Examples would be August Bank Holiday, New Year's Day and Spring Bank Holiday.

**Bar billiards** - There is no equivalent in the US as far as I know. This is great pub game on a pool sized table but it's different. You have seven white balls and a red one. There are no pockets around the table but there are 9 holes in the table surface and three wooden mushrooms. The object is to shoot from one end of the table and get balls into the holes without hitting the mushrooms over, but after hitting another ball. It doesn't sound much but it is brilliant fun, especially after a couple of *pints* of *scrumpy*. Don't visit England without trying it at least once.

**BBC English** - BBC English is used by many people to mean the proper pronunciation of English words, or a standard accent. Recently, though, the BBC have completely ruined this by employing people with all sorts of regional accents, including cockneys who really don't talk proper at all mate!

**Beeb** - The Beeb is the nickname for the **BBC**, the British Broadcasting Company, our main TV company. We all pay a licence fee to watch the BBC but it does mean that there are no *ads* on their channels.

**Big dipper** - The big dipper is the **roller coaster**. However by American standards perhaps we should call them "little dippers" as yours are generally a little larger than ours! We also call the "plough" star system the "big dipper".

**Big Issue** - Walking around London you may well have rough looking people come up to you and shout "Big Issue". Try not to act alarmed - they are normally homeless people who make about a quarter for every issue they sell. You should buy one and help them out. The Big Issue magazine is there to talk about homeless issues and help homeless people make a buck - well a *quid* actually!

Chuck found it strange that all the waiters in the UK were called Bill.

**Bill** - Don't ask for a **check** at the end of a meal in the UK - you'll just confuse the waiter or waitress. They won't know whether you want a health check, spell check or a time check! Ask for the bill.

**Billiards** - A ball game with three balls, one red and two white, played on a table like a pool table but bigger. The original billiards table had no pockets and points were only scored by making cannons - making your white hit both other balls. Today's billiards tables have pockets, so that scores are made by cannons but also by pocketing a ball, after hitting any other ball.

**Billion** - Amazing isn't it. We have the same word for almost the same thing. In fact a billion in American is a thousand million but in English it is a **million million**, though recently we have started to use your version so as to avoid over generous tips.

**Biro** - A **ballpoint pen**. The most popular brand is Biro and now everyone calls every pen a Biro.

**Blighty** - Another word for **England**.

**Blinkers** - These are the things that horses wear to stop them seeing anywhere other than straight ahead. You call them **blinders**.

**Blu tac** - Blu tac is what you would call **poster putty**. However, we call all similar objects blu tac, whatever their real name is. Just like you do with Xerox machines and we do with *hoovers*!

**Boarding school** - These are the schools where kids live as well as learn. Some of them also take *day boys and girls*.

**Bob** - You still hear older folks talking about a couple of bob, meaning a couple of **shillings**. Nowadays a shilling would be five pence and a couple of bob would be ten pence. My Grandfather used to give me ten bob to buy sweets with. However, he was actually giving me fifty pence but was translating back about 20 years for his own benefit.

**Bob-a-job** - Even after decimalisation in the UK, bob-a-job lived on for many years. Once a year the cub scouts went around the village or town with their bob-a-job forms with the objective of doing little jobs for people for a bob a go, or 5 pence as it became. The problem with bob a job, even when I was a cub, was that the name didn't move with the times and some people took it a bit too literally. There was nothing worse than cleaning two cars, mowing the lawn, washing the windows then being given five pence by some *stingy* old *bloke*.

**Bonfire night** - Remember, remember the 5th of November. Gunpowder, treason and plot. Although Halloween originated in England, it is not celebrated as wildly here as it is in the US. But a week later, everyone in England lights a huge bonfire and sets off lots of fireworks and eats burgers, baked potatoes, hot dogs, *parkin* cake and all sorts of other goodies, huddled around the fire. Every community and many companies organise bonfires for those with no *garden*. It is all in celebration of Guy Fawkes who tried to blow up the houses of parliament. What a great thing to celebrate! A guy is burned on the fire, made by the kids from old clothes and stuffed with straw and paper. A guy is an effigy of a human. May be the forerunner to the famous Texas A&M bonfire!

**Booze cruise** - Booze is cheaper in France and it is worth the trip just to stock up on alcohol. The cheapest way to do this is to take one of the booze cruises offered by the ferry companies. Basically you and bunch of your buddies take the ferry to France, drinking all the way, stock up on booze in a French *hypermarket* (still drinking), then jump back on the ferry to England and do some more drinking. Generally sleep is avoided and if you feel unwell the side of the boat is very convenient. To be avoided!

**Brackets** - **Parentheses** to you. Or the things that hold shelves up!

**Car boot sale** - This has nothing to do with the boots you wear on your feet. A boot sale is where hundreds of people descend on a field with cars full of unwanted wedding presents, clothes and other junk. They set it all out on wallpaper pasting tables for the general public to come and buy. I did my first one recently, selling all my unwanted stuff from the boot of my Explorer - it started at 7:30am on a Sunday and the people were so eager to see what we had they were helping us unpack the boxes - nightmare! Still we made seventy *quid* from stuff we would have thrown away! It's like an outdoor **garage sale**.

**Carnival** - Every winter, thousands of people build floats that are pulled behind tractors, covered in lights, made up into all kinds of weird scenes to take part in the carnival. The event moves from town to town and takes place every night in the dark so that the scenes can be lit up. Tens or hundreds of floats will take part in a carnival. In the US it is called a **parade**.

**Carvery** - This is a British wonder. The best Sunday would consist of getting up late, trundling down to a remote country *pub* and having the carvery. This consists of roast joints of meat. There will be a whole turkey, a leg of pork (with the skin on, scored, salted and roasted HOT so that it turns into *crackling*), leg of lamb and a big piece of beef. This will all be accompanied by the usual apple sauce (pork), mint sauce (lamb) and *Yorkshire pudding* (beef) as well as roast potatoes, roast parsnips and other sundry vegetables with a large jug of *gravy*, made from the meat juices, in the pan it was roasted in. Mmmmmmm.

**Cashpoint machine** - **ATM** to you, cashpoint for short. This last year the banks have started to introduce charges to use ATMs from other banks - not a popular move.

**Casualty** - This is where you go in the hospital when you have an accident. You call it the **emergency room**. These days you also see A&E on the signs, which is short for Accident and Emergency.

**Catapult** - **Slingshot**. I was banned from having one as a child - I think it had to do with the amount of glass that got broken as a result.

**Chat show** - **Talk show** to you. Unlike Letterman and Leno, chat show hosts in the UK sometimes let the guests say something too!

**Chemist** - Don't go looking for a **drugstore** in England, you won't find one. But you will find a chemist. Most of them are set up just like Eckerds. I once heard a quiz programme on the radio in Austin where they asked what us Brits call a drugstore. The answer, apothecary, was accepted and the guy got a point. Get out of here! That was centuries ago.

**Cheque** - How we used to pay our bills in the old days, before electronic banking started. **Check** in the US. Banks provide them for free in the UK. I was amazed you pay for them in the US, but you do get to choose groovy designs.

**Christmas crackers** - These have never really taken off in the US, though I have seen them for sale in speciality shops from time to time. They are brightly decorated paper tubes with a handle at each end. You reach across the table and ask someone to pull the other end. When it breaks, a snapper gives out a loud bang, a party hat drops out along with a small gift and a terrible joke. We make our own - you get better gifts that way.

**Chrysanths** - We both shorten the word for **chrysanthemums**. Us to chrysanths and you to **mums**.

**Cinema** - **Movie theater** to you chaps.

**Coconut shy** - This is a side show you'll find at country *fairs* and *fetes*. You buy some wooden balls and throw them at coconuts on sticks. If you knock one down, you keep it!

**College** - We use this word to mean **university** as well as other higher education establishments.

**Comprehensive school** - If a kid didn't pass the *eleven plus* exam, they went to a *secondary modern school*, rather than a *grammar school* at the grand old age of eleven. I was in the last year of kids who sat the eleven plus. The system changed so that both types of school were replaced with an all encompassing comprehensive school. Same as your **high school**.

**Conkers** - This is the name of the **horse chestnut** and the children's game that uses them. To play conkers you thread your conker onto a shoelace with a knot in the end and take it in turns to hit your friend's conker then let him hit yours. The winner is the one whose conker does not break up. After beating one friend your conker is called a one-er. After beating two friends it is called a two-er, unless his had previously beaten another one in which case yours would be a three-er and so on. Treating your conker with drugs, heat or other secret strengthening tricks is strictly forbidden, punishable by death under UK law.

**Cot** - **Crib**. The thing baby sleeps in. Or not in our case!

**Counterfoil** - If you still use a cheque book in the UK, the bit that stays in the book is called the counterfoil. You might call it a **stub**.

**Course** - Apart from describing our sense of humour, a course is what you would call a **class**. I did a course in business at university.

**Cutlery** - Knives and Forks. Called **flatware** or **silverware** in the US (even if it's plastic!). Apparently there is more cutlery to go round in the UK as you always get clean cutlery after every course in a restaurant.

**CV** - This is what we call a **resumé**. It is actually short for the latin, Curriculum Vitae, meaning "the course of life".

**Daddy long legs** - This has nothing to do with your father. It is what we call a **crane fly**, though never to their face, of course!

**Day boys/girls** - These are the kids who attend *boarding schools*, but rather than live there too, they attend each day just like other schools.

**Desmond** - A desmond is a lower second class honours degree. Our honours degrees are ranked (from best to worst) as a first class (a first, for short), an upper second (two-one for short), lower second (two-two or desmond for short) and a third. You can also get a non-honours and a pass, but you might not own up to them!! Desmond comes from Desmond Tutu (two-two, get it?).

**Direct debit** - How utility companies take payments direct from our bank accounts with the ability to change the amount. They simply divide your annual spend by twelve and take that amount each month. One reason why we don't need cheques in the UK. Similar to your **electronic funds transfer**.

**Directory enquiries** - When you call 192 from a British phone a nice person will welcome you to directory enquiries. They look up phone numbers for you. It would be **directory assistance** or **information** in America.

**Dirty weekend** - These are highly recommended. A dirty weekend is one where you and your partner (or someone else's partner) disappear for a couple of days for rampant sex.

**Dodgem cars** - Generally shortened to "dodgems", these little electric cars at the fair are called **bumper cars** in America.

**Doodle bug** - Both my parents and my grandparents hid from the doodle bugs in the war. They were the flying bombs that Hitler sent over to England during the war. Apparently you called them **buzz bombs**!

**Dosh** - This is a fairly common word for **money**.

**Draughts** - **Checkers** to you.

**Drawing pin** - **Thumbtack** to you chaps.

**Drink up** - In a pub, 10 minutes before closing time you will hear the barman shout "last orders please". This tells you to get the last round in before it is too late. When the clock strikes 11pm, they will then shout "time" to tell you it is too late to order any more. You now have 20 minutes to drink up after which time it is illegal to drink. This is called "drinking up time".

**Dummy** - **Pacifier** for a baby. Also the **mannequin** in a clothing shop window or **someone who has no brain**.

**Egg timer** - You would call this an **hour glass**. Presumably your eggs are bigger than ours if they take an hour to cook!

**Elastoplast** - If you cut yourself you would put a *plaster* or elastoplast on it. Or to give it it's full name, a sticking plaster. In America you have **band aids**. Elastoplast is just a brand name that sometimes gets used instead of *plaster*.

**Eleven plus** - This is the name of the exam that eleven year olds used to sit to determine if they went to *grammar school* or a *secondary modern school*. Often the first exam a kid ever sat.

**Elevenses** - Elevenses is an old fashioned habit with us Brits. It consists of stopping work for a *cuppa* and a *bickie* at around eleven in the morning, before carrying on till lunch time. Most people don't have time for elevenses any more though.

**Eurovision song contest** - Every year a terrible thing happens on TV right across Europe. One lucky unknown singer from each country vies for the title. The object is to unite Europe - which it does. Everyone in every country seems to hate it equally. 1998 was won by a transvestite! Super!

**Fag** - Probably the most famous troublesome word for Brits in the USA. I even fell for it myself when I visited my first US supermarket aged 16 and asked how much the fags were. The lady gave me a horrible stare and pretended not to hear me. Little did she know I thought I had found a business opportunity to make money on **cigarettes**. Fags are expensive here!

Charles casually asks if he can bum a fag.

**Fair** - **Carnival** to you. Swings and roundabouts, big wheels and other rides amongst the hot dog and *candyfloss* stands. We also have country fairs which are similar to yours with crafts and arts and sometimes animal displays and the like.

**Fancy dress** - Fancy dress means dressing up in a **costume**. Probably to go to a fancy dress party. In America that would be a **costume party**. In our office we can come to work in casual dress on Fridays. You often hear people saying to each other "Oh I didn't realise it was fancy dress today". That is British humour for you, *taking the mickey* out of people with loud shirts and wacky clothes.

**Fete** - **Field day**. Most schools and villages have a fete in the summer with side-shows, games, races, food and drink and a *coconut shy*.

**Film** - We don't go to the movie theatre to see a **movie**. We go to the *pictures* (or *cinema*) to see a film.

**Finals** - Your finals are the final exams you do at university. Possibly the worst few weeks of your life. We don't have **grade points** - the result of your degree is generally dependant on the results of your finals. Some courses use continual assessment or coursework to avoid this process but finals do avoid the problem of having people study for hundreds of years collecting points and getting a degree when, frankly, they don't deserve one.

**First floor** - The *lift* always starts on the ground floor and goes up to the first then the **second floor** etc. If you want an upstairs room in an English motel, it may well be on the first floor. I had a huge argument the first time I went to Florida and wanted a ground floor room. When I was told my room was on the first floor I almost hit the guy. I think the feeling was mutual!

**Fiver** - A fiver is a **five pound note**. Our notes are all a different colour and different size. This, along with subtle but bold shapes on each note, helps partially sighted people and blind people to handle money as well as the rest of us. It's fun to watch Brits trying to figure out different dollar bills to avoid giving $100 tips!

**Flannel** - If you ask for a flannel in a British house you will be given a **washcloth** for your face.

**Football** - **Soccer** to you. The national sport. Both on and off the field sadly! At school, usually called footy or footer.

**Form** - This is the way we describe which **grade** we are in at school. In a normal school you would start at age eleven in the first form (or the first year). You would finish in the fifth form (or fifth year) and optionally stay on for two more years to do your *A-levels*. These two years are called the lower sixth and the upper sixth. Sixth formers are the ones that study a bit harder because they generally chose to be there!

**Fresher's ball** - During your first year at university you would be referred to as a fresher. Every year there is a ball for the freshers to get to know each other. And, of course, the experienced students take the opportunity to check out the new *talent*!

**Fringe** - The front of your hair - your **bangs**! Makes Brits smile for some reason, when you say "bangs"!

**Fringe** - The fringe in theatre land is the equivalent of **off broadway** in the USA. The most famous fringe is at the Edinburgh Festival, where some of the finest new acts are to be seen.

**Fruit machine** - **Slot machine** to you. The fruit machines in Las Vegas are like the ones we had in the UK about 15 years ago. You pull the handle and watch the reels spin. If you win you win. If you don't you don't. Boring! Since gambling is permitted everywhere in the UK (within certain guidelines), it has developed a lot further than this. In order to keep the gambling public happy, machines now have features galore. It is not enough to match fruit symbols now, there are up nudges, down nudges, combination nudges, additional features to the reels, entire electronic games kicked off by features, held features, win gambles, win swops for features, feature exchanges and so on. Most 10 year olds can work these things and make pocket money by helping grown-ups work out what happened when everything starts flashing and helping them to win. Truly amazing. Makes the Vegas machines seem a bit boring though!

**Full stop** - **Period** to you. In English, period really only means the thing a woman has every month. Which is why Brits snigger when you say it.

**Gangway** - This is the gap between rows of seats, where one can walk - like in a restaurant. Or it's the thing you walk up onto a ship. Finally if you want a crowd to move out of the way because you are coming through, you would shout "gangway" at the top of your voice - try it outside Buckingham Palace next time you are there.

**GCSE** - General Certificate of Secondary Education. These are the exams that students in their 5th year of secondary school take when they are 16. After these, students may leave school or go onto the 6th form where they spend two more years studying for their *A-levels*, which are university entrance exams.

**Grammar school** - When these existed they were the schools that brighter kids went to at age 11. To get to grammar school meant passing the *eleven plus* exam.

**Guide dog** - **Seeing eye dog** to you chaps. I still don't know why American drive up ATM machines have braille keys. Do seeing eye dogs drive in the USA? In the UK they only walk!

**Gum** - Gum means **glue** in the UK. When you want to buy some chewing gum, be careful or you may find yourself sticking your teeth together.

**Handbag** - A woman carries a handbag. A man will never understand the contents of one. You call them **purses**, which is confusing for us because a *purse* is something that goes in the handbag and contains money.

**Hen night** - The equal and opposite of the *stag night*. Naturally girls are worse but still manage to blame it all on the chaps. **Bachelorette party**!

**High Street** - When I was a kid you always went shopping to the High Street. In fact every town in the country was built around the High Street as the centre of activity and shopping. Today though, the High Streets are quiet and the traders who occupy them are finding it more difficult to stay in business as the supermarkets and other shops are moving out of town.

**High Street shops** - This is a term you will hear in the UK which refers to the **national chains** of shops that you would expect to find in every town's High Street. Sadly these days with the move to out of town shopping centres (Malls) these shops are moving out of the High Streets and leaving them somewhat desolate.

**Hole in the wall** - Another expression for *cashpoint machine* or **ATM** to you chaps.

**Holiday** - **Vacation** to you. We usually go on a two-week holiday every summer since the basic holiday entitlement in the UK is 4 or 5 weeks when you start work. We also get several *bank holidays*.

**Hoover** - Really a brand of **vacuum cleaner** but the word "hoover" is used to describe all vacuum cleaners. Like you call all copy machines "Xerox machines". We don't Xerox something, we photocopy it. We use the hoover to do the hoovering.

**Hurling** - Apparently this one doesn't translate too well into American. Hurling is nothing to do with being sick, it is a sport, played a lot in Ireland which is like a cross between hockey and rugby. The players try to get a hard ball into, or over, a goal with the aid of a stick.

**Hypermarket** - Just when we thought supermarkets couldn't get any bigger they invented the hypermarket. It is basically a huge **supermarket**. There are a lot of them on the north coast of France that the Brits visit to buy huge volumes of cheap booze.

**Insects** - We don't use the word **bugs** like you do. We either refer to insects by name (Charles, Henry, Elizabeth - no I mean ants, spiders, moths etc) or just call them insects.

**Jasper** - Jasper is another word for **wasp**. You might also call them **yellow jackets**. They invade picnics in the summertime and usually end their lives in a pot of *jam*!

**Johnny** - Short for "rubber johnny", this is a term for a **condom**. We don't call them **rubbers**. Those are found on the end of pencils to rub out mistakes!

**Kiss gate** - If you wander across many of Britain's public footpaths, out in the country, you are likely to come across a kiss gate. These gates are designed to let people through but to keep animals in the fields. Only one person can get through at a time and the man is supposed to go first. In order for the lady to follow, the man has to let the gate go back, but not until he gets a kiss! Cute huh? Excellent excuse on a first date!

Charles was determined to make friends during his trip to England.

**Ladybird** - **Ladybug**. Not even closely related to a bird! Does fly though.

**Last orders** - In a British pub you will hear someone shout "last orders", ten minutes before closing time. It's your last chance to order another beer before the bar closes.

**Lead** - The thing that a British dog uses to drag you along the street behind it. American dogs use a **leash**!

**Leaving do** - Another type of *do*. When someone leaves a company, their colleagues may arrange a leaving do for them. You might call it a **going away party** or **leaving party**.

**Letter box** - This is the **mail box** - big and red and found loitering on street corners.

**Licence fee** - In order to watch any TV in the UK you must pay a licence fee to the BBC. It's cheaper than your basic US cable package and gets you our five main channels. It means there are no *ads* on the BBC channels which is excellent. We also have cable and satellite TV channels at an extra cost and so our TV is getting more like yours, sadly.

**Lie-in** - Most normal people will have a lie-in on a Saturday and/or Sunday morning. Usually with a cup of tea and sometimes with the newspaper. It means to **lay in bed** until you feel so guilty you have to get up.

**Lift** - The American **elevator**. In England we don't talk in the lift, unless we are with close friends or colleagues. Even then, as soon as someone else steps in, all conversation stops! In America, these rules do not apply. Americans in England should attempt to abide by the English lift laws, or may accidentally upset the natives, who will be giving each other strange looks! A lift is also something you get by standing at the side of main roads with your thumb out. Americans hitch-hiking in the UK should avoid asking for a "ride"! This could result in some unplanned sexual activity with someone you have never met before!

**Local** - Your local is the **pub** you visit the most. It actually doesn't have to be the one that is nearest to you. So if you hear someone saying that they are "off down the local" you know where they are going.

**Lounge bar** - When I was a kid, most pubs had a *saloon bar* and a lounge bar. The price of a pint was a penny or two more in the lounge and, unlike the *saloon*, it had proper carpets and comfortable seating.

**Marks and Sparks** - This is how many people would refer to the country's leading retailer **Marks and Spencer**. Most people still seem to buy their underwear from M&S. Americans always snigger at the sign for men's briefs!

**Marquee** - This is the large **tent** that many people would rent to hold the party after a wedding.

**Maths** - This is what you call **math**. It is short for mathematics, the study of numbers. What I want to know is what you have done with the "s".

**Mobile** - These days everyone has a mobile. You chaps called them **cellular phones**. They were originally for talking but nowadays they send e-mails and surf the internet too. Whatever next?

**Naughts and crosses** - What everyone does in boring classes/meetings etc - **tic tac toe** in America.

**Note** - A note is what we call our paper money. We don't call them **bills**. For example a five pound note is called a *fiver* and a ten pound note is called a *tenner*. Strangely a twenty is called a twenty.

**O-Level** - At 16, school kids used to take around ten O-levels (O for Ordinary). These were the qualifications that got you into the sixth form, where you studied for your *A-levels* (A for Advanced). O-levels have been replaced by *GCSEs* which cover a broader range of educational ability (General Certificate of Secondary Education).

**Over the moon** - If you are over the moon about something it means you are **delighted**.

**Oxbridge** - A short way of referring to **Oxford and Cambridge** universities. When you are at school and planning your university applications you would say you were applying to Oxbridge if you were applying to both. Either way, you are a *smart arse*!

**Pantomime** - A Christmas tradition with no American equivalent. A pantomime is a show which takes normally mature, serious actors and actresses and sees them dressing up as members of the opposite sex to amuse children with popular stories. Usually has an evil man, a man dressed in drag as a widow and a dashing young male hero (really a woman in green tights). You spend most of your time shouting "It's behind you" and adults pretend they only go for the kids. A really disorganised event may also be described as something of a pantomime!

**Parcel** - This is what you call a **package**. For some strange reason it is always so much more exciting to receive a parcel than a letter.

**Pay packet** - This is what you get at the end of the week or month with a wodge of money in it. You call it a **pay check**. These days, of course, many people are paid electronically.

**Pay rise** - Not something you see very often - you would call this a **raise**.

**Pence** - The one hundred pennies that make up a British pound are called pence. The same as you have **cents**. However, you will often hear people calling them "p". So if you are asked for 50p you are expected to hand over fifty pence.

**Penny farthing** - I used to see an old chap cycling up and down our village street every day on a penny farthing. They are an amazing sight. You might call them **high-wheelers**, they are old bicycles with one huge wheel at the front and a tiny one at the back. When our currency had pennies and farthings the name would have made a lot of sense!

**Photocopier** - **Copier** or **Xerox machine** to you. If you ask someone where you can Xerox something in England, expect a blank stare - you need to ask where you can make a photocopy.

**Pictures** - As kids we spent a lot of time at the pictures. It is another word for the *cinema* or the **movie theater**.

**Pillar box** - My Mum always used to send me to the pillar box to post the letter. It is another word for *postbox* or as you would say, **mailbox**.

**Plaster** - If you cut yourself you would put a plaster on it. Or to give it it's full name, a sticking plaster. In America you have **band aids**.

**Polystyrene** - **Styrofoam** in the US. Same uses in both countries though we do have something against drinking tea or coffee out of polystyrene cups. It's just not cricket!

**Polytechnic** - This a kind of **technical college**. If you didn't get the grades to get into university, the second choice was to go to poly or polytechnic. Their degrees were the same as universities, but it was easier to get into them. Most polys are now converted to universities.

**Pompey** - I went to poly in Pompey. It is the colloquial slang for **Portsmouth**.

**Pontoon** - Also known as **21** or **blackjack** where you have to get 21 to beat the bank.

**Post** - The **mail**. The post arrives in the morning in the UK. It drops through your letter box onto your hall carpet. You can read it in bed before you go to work, with a nice *cuppa*. Very civilised.

**Post mortem** - **Autopsy** in American. Not a fun job in either language.

**Postbox** - Where you post things. They are on street corners as well as at the post office. You'd call them a **mailbox**.

**Postcode** - **Zipcode** to you chaps. Postcodes are in the form RG26 5AN where the first two letters tell you the main postal town (RG=Reading) and the rest narrows down your house to the nearest 6 houses. That means that with just your house number and postcode anything can be delivered anywhere in the UK. Many mail order companies just ask you your house number and postcode - the rest is printed by computer. Clever huh! The new 9 digit US zip codes will achieve the same thing.

**Postman** - This is the chap who delivers your post on his bike or his little red van. He will sign for stuff that you are supposed to sign for if he misses you and hide it in the *garden* and leave a note for you! Ours dresses up like *Father Christmas* at Christmas time.

**Pram** - Like a big **stroller**, sometimes the top lifts off the wheels and can be used as a cot. That would then be called a carry cot. Short for perambulator.

**Premium bonds** - These are a **government savings scheme** that pay no interest. No - we're not all completely mad - instead of interest they pay out millions in prize money each month and keep their value exactly the same. In these days where bank interest rates are so low - they suddenly become a much more interesting way of saving! It's like a lottery where each ticket lasts a lifetime or until you cash them in. Cool huh!

**Prep school** - Short for preparatory school, this is the school that kids go to before they go to *public school*. Normally from ages eight to thirteen.

**Primary school** - From the age of 5 until 11, our kids go to primary school.

**Property** - We generally use the word "property" where you would say **real estate**. To us - that sounds like the opposite of "pretend estate" - like Disneyworld perhaps!

**Pub** - The cornerstone of British social life. Every village has a pub, or several. These tend to be friendly sociable places to go for a pie and *pint*, meet the locals, get a cheap meal and drink some of that nice British beer, we know you like so much. They usually have a beer garden and maybe a skittle alley, pool table and always a fruit machine or two. Town and city pubs come in several varieties. There are the drinking men's pubs, where the guys who leave the missus at home go, to chat to their *mates* and have a *fag*. There are the trendy, loud, expensive yuppie pubs. There are the family pubs which have separate rooms where kids can go, and they have lots of food and a playground (yuck!), and then there are the nice ones.

**Pub crawl** - Not quite as literal as it sounds, a pub crawl consists of drinking a pint at as many different pubs as possible, one after the other. Towards the end of the evening the "crawl" bit starts to take effect. Often followed by a *curry*! And more pints of course! Similar to your **bar hopping**.

**Public convenience** - You may still see "public convenience" signs around England. They are pointing you to the nearest public *toilet* or **restroom**.

**Public school** - Rather oddly, this is the name we give our **private schools**. For those that can afford to opt out of the state education system, this would be the alternative.

**Purse** - A woman carries a purse to contain her money - notes and coins. I think you call this a **wallet** or a **pocket book**.

**Pushchair** - **Stroller** in American.

**Pylon** - This is what we would call a **high tension tower** which carries 11,000 volts of electricity.

**Queue** - Brits have never stood in **line**. But they have queued - at the post office, the deli, in traffic. We like to queue almost as much as you like to **stand in line**.

**RAF** - The **Royal Air Force** - our answer to Top Gun!

**Railway** - We refer to the **railroad** as a railway.

**Rates** - Rates are **local taxes**. Currently based on the value of your property, they are generally lower than your property tax and are payable monthly. For some strange reason this is the only bill payment that is only paid in 10 months of the year - maybe the council find dividing by twelve too difficult! Rates are now called "council tax" here in the UK.

**Reception** - This is the area in a hotel or business that you would call the **front desk** or the **lobby**.

**Red Arrows** - This is the name of the Royal Air Force aerobatic display team. Very similar to your US Air Force **Thunderbirds**.

**Return** - When you want to buy a **round trip** ticket, when visiting England, ask for a return.

**Revise** - Before an exam, we would revise the subject. I remember spending many unhappy hours revising for my *A-Levels*. You might **review** your subjects in a similar situation or simply **study**.

**Rise** - You call this a **raise**. Not a common occurrence in either place, sadly! Also called a *payrise*.

**Rounders** - This is a game that kids play, which has almost exactly the same rules as **baseball**.

**Rubber** - In England you would never hesitate to borrow an old rubber from a good friend, or even a stranger, for that matter. They would probably have one on the end of their pencil. Most kids chew their rubbers then break them into pieces and throw them at each other. You call them **erasers**! This caused me immense embarrassment the first time I tried to borrow one in the US.

**Rubber Johnny** - This is a term for a **condom**. Usually shortened to just Johnny.

**Saloon** - When I was a kid, most pubs had a saloon bar and a *lounge bar*. The price of a pint was cheaper in the saloon and the decor was more your spit and sawdust style. The labourers drank in the saloon. These days both bars have been knocked into one and everyone shares everything.

**School** - This is either primary school (ages 5 to 11) or secondary school (ages 11 to 18).

**Secondary school** - Short for secondary modern school, this is what you call **high school**. In the UK, if you failed your *eleven plus* exam, this is the kind of school you would go to instead of a *grammar school*. After this system changed to the current one, both these kinds of schools were replaced by *comprehensive schools*.

**Sellotape** - This is a brand of **scotch tape**, but we use it to describe all sticky tapes.

**Semi** - Short for a semi-detached house or a **duplex** in the US. If someone is being a bit dim you might also say they are semi-detached.

**Serviette** - Or "servie-what"? as I once heard in a Texas restaurant! I should have asked for a **napkin**!

**Set down** - You may see signs around London saying "set down only". This means you may only stop the car *momentarily* to **drop off** your passengers. No parking is allowed.

**Shares** - **Stocks** in a company are called shares.

**Shop** - **Store**. We go shopping, presumably you go storing? We will go to the shops the same way you will go to the mall. We don't have many malls, though they are beginning to appear. Some of them are created by putting a roof over an entire town centre - like the one in Camberley.

**Shopping trolley** - **Shopping cart**. These are used for collecting your shopping as you go around the supermarket. They also have another use, which to this day, is still unexplained. They have a habit of turning up in rivers. In fact, anywhere there is a large or medium amount of water, there will be a shopping trolley. Nobody knows why. They are usually many miles from the nearest supermarket. I'm not sure if the same phenomenon has reached America yet. What is the difference between a shopping trolley and a policeman? (or whoever else you like). Answer: the shopping trolley has a mind of it's own!

**Shove-halfpenny** - Pronounced "shove hape-knee", this is a an old pub game where you push polished coins, old halfpennies, along a polished board to score points. Still around in a few pubs but mostly replaced by newer games that take your money quicker.

**Skip** - What do you call a Skoda with a sunroof? Answer - a skip! In the UK, Skoda used to be the car to laugh about, cheap, ugly and nobody would be seen dead in one. A skip is a **dumpster** so now maybe the joke makes sense.

**Skipping rope** - **Jump rope** - no sane person would use one!.

**Sledge** - This what you would call a **sled**. We go sledging when you go sledding.

**Snooker** - Also played on a large table, with pockets. There are 15 reds and 6 other coloured balls, each with a different value. Players take it in turns to use the white to pocket a red, then a colour then a red and so on. Once the reds are all gone, the colours have to be pocketed one by one in the order yellow (2), green (3), brown (4), blue (5), pink (6) and black (7). Highest break is 147. Pool is also played but mainly in *pubs*.

**Spondulicks** - Another word for your **money**. This one dates back to the last century but the origin remains unknown. Some people say "spondulies".

**Stag night** - Before you get married, you and your buddies go out on a stag night, or a stag weekend. The object being to get as drunk as possible before the happy day, hoping to meet a bunch of girlies on a *hen night*! You call it a **bachelor party**.

**Stand for election** - This is what we do when you **run for office**.

**Standing order** - How utility companies etc take payments direct from our accounts without being able to change the amount. Cheques are not used much in England any more, just for giving your friends money. You may call it an **electronic funds transfer** or EFT.

**Stone** - When I told the man in the driving licence office I was 13 stone 10, he said that it must be close to a boulder! Very funny! A stone is **14 pounds** which makes me about 192 pounds. Big enough to hit him!

**Strimmer** - **Weed eater** or **trimmer** in the US. A weed eater in the UK would be something like a cow or a goat! My American friend's house rental contract obliged him to "Weed eat the yard on a regular basis". In English this would cause stomach ache and possibly other illnesses!

**Surgery** - Apart from what happens in an operating theatre, we also call the local **doctor's office**, the surgery. Also, when members of parliament hold meetings for members of the public to raise questions with them, they often call them surgeries.

**Swimming baths** - We say we are off to the swimming baths when we are going to the **swimming pool**. We use both expressions to mean the same thing.

**Telephone box** - That lovely old red thing you see on every British street corner. Or did until they were mostly replaced by modern phone booths. BT sold them off at a hundred quid each - now they are collectors items. Most drunks miss them as somewhere to pee after the curry! Called **phone booths** in America.

**Telephone directory** - We don't use the expression **white pages** like you do. We just refer to the telephone directory. However, we do talk about yellow pages in the same way as you.

**Tenner** - A tenner is a **ten pound note**. Our notes are all a different colour and different size. This, along with subtle but bold shapes on each note, helps partially sighted people and blind people to handle money as well as the rest of us. So if you are asked for a tenner in England - get out your *dosh*, not a fat man with a good singing voice!

**Tick** - When we fill in forms we are asked to tick the boxes. You **check** the boxes. When putting a tick in the box - be careful not to confuse this with the little biting insect, which is also called a tick!

**Timber** - Don't ask for **lumber** in England. Lumber is either a lolloping walk or the lower part of your back. Timber is any kind of treated wood. It is also something a lumberjack shouts when the tree starts to topple.

**Time** - The word "time" is the same in both countries. However the way we tell it is different. When I was first asked the time in a shopping mall in Austin I said it was "half ten". The very confused guy just looked at me and said "What, five o'clock?". We say "half ten" for **ten thirty**. We say "quarter past ten" when you would say **quarter after ten** or, more likely **ten fifteen**. We say "quarter to ten" when you would say **quarter of ten**.

**Tippex** - This is another brand name for a correction fluid. However, we generally say "tippex" in the same way that you say **white out**, which is your equivalent. Ours is a little thicker in texture.

**Tire** - Something you do when you are worn out or *knackered*. Best thing to do is to go to bed.

**Torch** - We uses torches when we go camping to see in the dark, in our tents. My American friends didn't believe we would do anything so dangerous. But that's because we were talking about **flashlights**, not a flaming stick!

**Trolley** - When you arrive at the airport the first thing you'll need is a trolley. Don't be tempted to ask for a **cart**.

**Tube** - The London underground system is called the tube. You have a **subway** in New York. In England it is also called the *underground*.

**TV licence** - These are the licences we buy in order to watch TV legally in the UK. There are detector vans that roam the country looking for TVs that are switched on at addresses that have not purchased a TV licence. If you are caught - you are made to watch TV commercials - because the licence fee means we don't have commercials on the BBC. Yippee!

**TV programme** - This is what we call a **TV show**, though you will hear both phrases used here these days.

**Tyre** - The rubber based thing that goes on a wheel. It is illegal to guarantee 50,000 mile usage in the UK as these tyres contain less rubber and more nylon. Nylon doesn't stick to wet roads, hence the usual pile-ups on I35 when it rains. **Tire** to you.

**Underground** - The underground is another word for the **subway** or as we like to call it, the tube.

**University** - Age 18 to 21 or so. You say **school**. Basically still free, entry being based on merit and exam results, rather than money. However, the government is gradually sneaking in more costs for students and it is unlikely to remain free for much longer, I fear.

**VAT** - **Value added tax** or **sales tax** in the US. The main difference is ours is included in the price you see, so nothing gets added at the till.

**Wad** - If you had a big fat wad, you would have loads of **money**.

**Wallet** - When I was 16 I had my wallet stolen in Boston airport. I was worried when the announcement on the plane was about a missing **pocket book**. But no. That's what you call a wallet. I also heard it called a **bill fold**.

**Wash up** - We do this after dinner and you do it before. We are talking about **doing the dishes** whereas you are talking about your hands!

**Way out** - I had to laugh recently when I was at the *pictures* with an American friend. She asked me what was outside that was so "way out"! There was a door with "way out" illuminated above it. It actually means **exit**, not that there is something groovy and way out through there.

**WC** - I'm often asked by my American chums about the good old WC. It is never said but often seen on signs, not just in England but all across Europe. It is short for "water closet" and simply means the *loo*, *toilet* or **restroom**.

**Wedge** - Your wedge, like your *wad* is another expression for your **money**.

**White horse** - Around Wiltshire there are a number of white horses. They are cut into the hillside and are visible from miles around. In fact, if you are visiting Stonehenge there is a leaflet there that describes a three hour driving tour of about 6 or 7 local white horses. Worth a visit on a sunny day. The reason they are white is that below the top soil the area is made of white chalk.

**Wonga** - Your wonga is your *wad*, or in other words your **money**.

**Year** - At school we refer to the **grades** as *forms* or years. We call the first year, "the first year". Cryptic huh? We also call it the "first form". We also use years to describe our progress through university.

# Index

## C

## D

## E



## F

## K



## L



## M



## N



## O

## T